Richey's

To: Marcus —

Of Home Sales

"Remember the ABC's of Selling— "Always Be Closing!" Thank you

'Medal of Honor' stories about selling the American Dream

for your help on the PRIMA,

Best Regards,

Tom Richey

By Thomas W. Richey

MIRM, CAASH

Richey Resources

www.richeyresources.com

Printed by

Mercury Print Productions, Inc.
50 Holleder Parkway
Rochester, NY 14615
1.888.777.7468
www.mercuryprint.com

Printed in the United States of America

First Edition: January 2010

ISBN: 978-0-9817405-5-3

Acknowledgements

It is only fitting to acknowledge the long line of incredibly professional salespersons I have been blessed to know and work with over the years. Their inner strength, enduring positive mental attitude, thirst for knowledge, and capacity to consistently close sales has been inspiring. Hats off to them! They are, without a doubt, the engine that drives the new and resale home selling industry. They are the Gods of Valhalla, the Spartans, the high achievers in an industry that focuses all too often on "things" not "people."

Here's to you – master closers – You are the true icons of the Housing Hall of Fame.

I would like to acknowledge the brains behind the enterprise, our hard working associate, Danielle Fyffe. Without her incredible word processing skills, layout creativity, artistic jiggle-jaggle, and untowardly perseverance, this book would never have happened.

When distributing accolades, one must mention the team of sales managers – men and women – that hire, train, motivate, and monitor their superstars. Without them, there would be no ticket to write and no bar to raise.

Other acknowledgements go to proof reader, Sheila Decker, for her attention with the minutest details.

Last, but certainly not least, this book would never have happened without the brainstorm and prodding of a young, rising sales star from Las Cruces, New Mexico – Quint Lears. He suggested there was a need for a collection of award winning sales stories to motivate everyone who awakens each morning to the inner self that cries, "Where is your next sale coming from?" Quint was the inspiration to get this book into motion, execution, and final completion. If we had an abundance of Quint Lears selling homes, we'd be celebrating record years of sales and profits.

Finally, I acknowledge YOU, the reader. You are a team of one, who in concert with your peers around the country, will be instrumental in bringing the housing industry to a new level of expertise. Remember, every time a home is sold, 278 related goods and services impact the U.S. economy which contributes to enhanced jobs for our nation.

Good luck and good hunting.

Tom Richey

A Salute to Sales Professionals

In the United States of America, new home sales practitioners have...

Benched more home sites
Poured more concrete
Dug more dirt
Set more forms
Cut more lumber
Framed more walls
Wired more electrical
Carried more hod
Laid more brick
Installed more insulation
Hung more sheetrock
Painted more rooms
Laid more flooring
Set more doors
Sealed more windows
Sold more appliances
Connected more plumbing
Nailed more roofing
Seeded more yards
Financed more mortgages

... and fulfilled more dreams than any other sales breed in America!

~Tom Richey

Introduction

The Congressional Medal of Honor is the highest honor that can be bestowed upon a military hero. In this vein, I have reflected on the professional "Medal of Honor" sales persons I have known over the years and have assembled a collection of their inspirational stories. The people and their deeds were a great motivator to me, and I know they will be to you as well. Let us all remember that something wonderful happens when a professional salesperson sells the American Dream.

It's high time we commemorate the men and women who sell new and resale homes! For years, housing sales people have been the forgotten soldiers of the home selling wars. If you sell and close you win; if you don't you lose. It's as simple as that! The housing industry must understand there is absolutely no substitute for a highly trained and motivated salesperson. And, we should bend over backwards to celebrate their victories and accomplishments.

Most salespersons are sold on their product, but now it's time for everyone in sales to be sold on the enterprise as a professional career. It's time we extol our salespeople who may be the hardest working taskmasters in any industry.

Nothing happens in the housing business until a home is sold. Sure, we have the professionals called engineers who design the land plans, architects who do a magnificent job of creating floor plans, developers who make magic with their bulldozers, constructors who know how to pour concrete, frame a home, and insulate a home, build GREEN, and finish to a tenth of a decimal point. We have the very best trades in the world. But remember, a home will stand empty if a highly trained and motivated selling practitioner is not there to close a contract.

It's time we took back sales – and that means putting selling in the perspective it deserves, the professional perspective. Is it more worthy to be an attorney, a doctor, a CPA? Let us suggest it is equally important to be the consummate professional in an occupation that creates more jobs than any other single business in this country. If you want the answer to job creation, look to the housing industry.

And, let us remember, selling is a trying job. You don't "try" real estate, real estate tries you. It can be long hours of boredom followed by moments of crisis when two families enter the sales office at one time. There can be rude customers, short time frames to finance and complete a sale, misinformed management, a non competitive price list, and sometimes consumer confidence that is in the tank. All in all, selling can be a hugely rewarding but also taxing endeavor.

Selling is a right brain exercise. Sales professionals are social animals that revel in helping people. They understand that the essence of selling is its alternatives and that time has no worth when one is not face-to-face with a prospect.

Selling is multi-dimensional. You have to find prospects, qualify them, tour them, present to them, be patient with them, overcome objections, and be consistent and persistent at closing, while refraining from being pushy, egotistical, or demanding. Sometimes builders have a hard time understanding the pressures and dynamics of selling.

Why does Mary have a better conversion rate? Or, why did Jimmy lose that sale? Or, is my salesperson working smarter or just harder? All these are indigenous to a career track that is mercurial at best. While we build homes to blueprints, we don't close buyers to finites. Every sale is different; every sale runs on a different track. No two home sales are ever the same.

To get the most out of this book, we suggest you first read it in a cursory fashion. Check off the Medal of Honor presentations that are most helpful and inspiring. Then, come back and read them in depth. Think about them. Evaluate how you can use the moral or message to your advantage. Then, come back and read them again. Highlight passages; practice the wordage. Remember, these super stars are just like you. If they can do it, you can do it. And, remember something else. All of us in home sales are the stewards of the American Dream. We are at the cutting edge of a profession that drives the U.S. economy. We have the pleasure and privilege to sell the American Dream. What could be more rewarding than the buyer who says, "Thank you so much for helping us improve our lives!"

These cursory chronicles go as far back as fifty years. In some cases, only first names are used since the sales professionals have disappeared from the housing scene. How sad! Wouldn't it be rewarding to have each and every one assembled around a blazing campfire embellishing their epic tales?

Yes, it's time to praise and eulogize salespeople. It's time we pray for them -- their motivation, skills enhancement, positive mental attitude, bulldog tenacity, confidence in the country, their company, and their own selves. We must pray for them so they make those extra attempts at writing business. Pray for them so they hear their buyers say, "Thank you so much for making our dreams come true, for being patient, and for showing us this was the right decision." Now more than ever, it's time to show our sales professionals love and respect.

Table of Contents

Story 1

Arriff

Persistence Pays

I used to write a newsletter for Stewart Title Company. It focused on new home sales. I would receive letters, notes, advisements, and telephone calls in the days before e-mail about all kinds of building, marketing, and selling events. Some were worthy of mention, most were not. Imagine my surprise when out of the mail pouch of random information came a letter from a happy owner to a salesperson who worked at an active adult, age restricted community in Annapolis, Maryland. The letter started out … "Dear Arriff – Ten years ago when we met you for the first time, we never thought we would buy a home from you. We visited you and your lovely community but felt we were not quite ready to purchase a home there."

The letter continued. "Several years later we came out again because we loved the ambiance, the cordiality of the people there, and the thought of making new friends. You took us on a magnificent tour as you did a few years back and kept us apprised of the progress of the development. Thank you for this."

The letter kept on. "Just a few years ago we were thinking about making a move to your community but had a financial setback. Last year a catastrophic event happened. We had an armed robbery in our house and felt it was time to move to a gated community. Mr. Arriff, we want you to know that if you had not continually called us on the phone to chat with us … sent us informative cards and notes, and genuinely made a friend of us, the chances are we would have forgotten about you and bought somewhere else. As a result, we came back and purchased your home, had a splendid move-in, made a ton of new friends, and are having the time of our life – thanks to you and your persistence."

Wow! Wow! Wow! Isn't that the best of all thank you letters? The power of this story is to stay in the follow up game and don't take yourself out of it until your prospects buy or they die.

Story 2

Eckert

In-home Selling at its Best

Eckert Mitchler was a one of a kind. He flew every light aircraft the German Luftwaffe had in World War II and came out without a scratch. He carried a packet of cyanide pills with him on every flight and was told that if he was forced to land in Russian occupied territory he must consume these pills to avoid torture. When he was flying night fighters at the end of the war, he was trained to put his plane down in the Allied zone where he would get better treatment as a prisoner of war. Twenty-eight years after the war, they still saluted him on the street! All of this experience served him well when he hired on board with Intermar -- The International Marketing Group to be its lead salesperson/sales manager in Germany selling U.S. and European property to the German market. Having hired and trained hundreds of German salespersons, I can attest to the

Germanic sales mentality. It is "my way or the highway." "I speak, you listen." "I lead, you follow." And of course, it is "Close this sale and give me the money now." Certainly, this is a hide-bound and high risk method of selling which buys a ton of cancellations. The challenge with Mitchler and the balance of the sales staff was to take this ego driven focus on making sales now and tone it down with a measure of empathy. Not an easy task! While Mitchler had the potential to be the German sales manager, we had to bridle his ego drive. I knew this after watching him perform an in-home sales presentation. In selling United States properties, Austrian ski condos, Swedish beach front properties, or properties in Spain all we had to do was bring people to closure in an in-home or in-office environment.

Mitchler would enter the home with bravado, bring the family together, instruct the head of household to hush the kids, escort everyone over to the dining room table, clean off the dishes and silverware, prop his selling tools at one end and proceed with his presentation. He was darn good at it and people listened. Perhaps it didn't hurt that he was a well-known war time folk hero. People would hug him in the halls or bow in reverence. World War II heroes were like rock stars in Germany at this time. The good news is once Mitchler learned the power of empathy and how to soften his presentation, he became an absolute master at leading people into a close. Sometimes these presentations reached far into the evening. A midnight or post midnight contract signing was not unusual. Families were fascinated by his presentations. He would take out the colored pictures, articulate the reasons why to buy in German, and slowly emphasize each and every purchasing point until the whole family agreed. He was one of the most patient salespersons ever. Yet, he was one of the most pleasurable. He learned how to inject personal anecdotes about his life, the good part of his military service, and even his relationship with his Maker. Mitchler was a master communicator once he learned the importance of empathy. In fact, I would put Mitchler into my Hall of Fame as one of the top ten salespersons I have ever observed – particularly on an in-home presentation. There was no question too small not to be heeded and no effort too large for him not to give his all. He was a 100% sales professional who lived, ate, and breathed sales!

The focal point of this story is that many sales people have a high degree of ego drive which is necessary to be a master closer. But, high ego drive and high pressure buy lots of cancellations and eventually wash out the sales professional. The secret is to have a balance between ego drive and empathy. Like a heat seeking missile shot from the ground, the missile tracks a drone in the sky. Through a series of ego drives (propulsions) and adjustments (empathies) the missile eventually locks onto the drone and shoots it down. Very similar to a master closer's presentation which, through a series of ego propulsions and empathy adjustments, eventually causes the objections to be neutralized and the sale to be closed. For the sales person, the lesson is to watch your ego. Don't let it get out of control.

Remember, the customer has what you require for the sale, dollars and desire. You have what the customer wants – a remarkable property. For sales managers, keep in mind that if sales people exhibit too much ego in their selling, they will lose. The balance of ego and empathy is absolutely required in the heat of the selling battle. You can train empathy, but you can't train ego.

Mitchler brought one other benefit to the table. As a former sales manager for the giant Investors Overseas Services (IOS) mutual fund company which was the largest mutual fund company at the time, he had a traffic-building form called "People I Know" worksheet. In 1967 IOS was a U.S. company that was importing more foreign dollars into the U.S. than any other single entity. It was worldwide in scope, and Mitchler was involved in its German operations.

One day, he put a form written in German on my desk and said, "This is the tool we use when we hire new salespersons at IOS. It is a form they fill out and use to make their first presentations and sales."

"Well, translate it for me, please."

Very carefully we went over this detailed worksheet, and I found out it consisted of twelve different categories that one's life touches with twenty blocks for names, addresses, and phone numbers. The new sales recruit sits down, reflects on his or her life, and fills in the form with the names of people they deal with in all walks of their life. For example, who they deal with in their car operations … their church affiliations ... their fraternal organizations ... who they know through their school ... who they know through friends and parents, and so on until every one of the twenty blocks in the twelve different life involvement categories is filled out. Then, the sales manager reviews the form with the new recruit and motivates that person to make cold calls on these people. It worked for the mutual fund and believe it or not, it works for home sales. We have translated this form into English and have offered it to many building companies across the U.S. Sadly, it has seldom been used. Why? Because we've had a surplus of traffic in the door and sales people did not have to reach into the world of sales prospecting. If traffic diminishes more, the *People I Know* form that was so generously given to me by Eckert Mitchler may come into vogue again. It should and must!

TOM TALKS... About What Makes a Salesperson Successful

Being Sociable: The ability to build relationships is key. And then close with the customer loving the process.

Having a Sense of Urgency: The capacity to inject believable urgency and move a sale to completion now! Above all, urgency must be believable.

Story 3

Sylvia

Quality vs. Quantity Selling

U.S. Home had a salesperson on its Florida staff named Sylvia. She was selling mature lifestyle buyers. There was some concern in sales management that she took too long upfront schmoozing her customers. It was not unusual for Sylvia to sit for fifteen or twenty minutes drinking coffee or soda with possible prospects. She resembled a mother hen spreading her figurative wings over her prospects as she wooed them into an open, not a closed mind. Perhaps she understood the basic selling principle of opening the mind to close the sale. And so it went!

Presentation after presentation included lengthy bonding and connecting time. When it came to touring the multi-model homes, the overall community, and the path to the close, Sylvia was an A.C.E* at maximizing her time with

---

* A.C.E. – **A**ccountable, **C**oncerned, **E**xpertised

prospects most likely to buy. In other words, she didn't waste any time touring deadbeats. To them she simply said, "Here is our brochure, tour our models, enjoy yourself. If you have any questions, come back and I'll be happy to help you." However, for the real qualifieds, Sylvia was off on a lengthy presentation which included a complete tour of the model homes, the community, the club house, the amenities, a ride in the golf cart on the course if necessary, on into the scenic impact areas, right down to a one-of-a-kind on a homesite. Then, it was back to the office for wrapping up the transaction. She knew how to *invest* her time. Management's concern about her upfront time allocation was quickly allayed when they pulled the numbers and found out that, although Sylvia was fronting fewer prospects than anybody else on the sales team, she was selling more net sales. It's a terrific argument for the quality not quantity approach to selling. Subsequently, she led her Florida sales staff for several consecutive years and took home all the sales awards.

Salespeople need to remember that every prospect is a buyer until proven otherwise. Only conversational counselling, deep discovery, a value-based presentation, and a one-of-a-kind close can determine who the buyers are and who the tryers are.

Don

The Master Closer

This vignette is about the power of ego drive and empathy. Most closers possess an abundance of ego but need to soften it with empathy. The dictionary defines empathy as the intellectual or imaginative apprehension of another's condition or state of mind without actually experiencing the feelings of the other. Sympathy on the other hand, is a feeling of compassion for another's sufferings with pity and commiseration.

Here's an example in sales. Empathy: I understand how you feel about losing your job, but as Will Rogers says, *"Don't wait to buy real estate; buy real estate and wait!"* Sympathy: I understand how you feel about losing your job. Here is my card. Give me a call when you're ready.

Too many salespeople embrace sympathy and lose countless sales over it. Empathy can be taught and trained. Look at this example.

The recreational land business attracted sales people from all walks of life and all levels of professionalism. There are many stories about the cast of characters that passed through that brief episode in real estate selling. One salesperson named Don worked for me selling camping projects in Texas. Don was the kind of salesperson whose type A profile drove him up the wall waiting for prospects. He would wait in anticipation for his next challenge outside the sales center. He would sing songs to psych himself up, recite his closing questions over and over, and literally paw the ground with his feet. If you've ever seen a bull in a pasture or even a thoroughbred waiting for the race to start, they often paw the ground with anticipation. This was Don's MO. Paw that ground with your feet until you dig a hole three inches deep. Paw and paw and paw and sell and sell and sell. Don, indeed, was a selling maverick, and a good one. Imagine my surprise many years later when I was working with a Pulte new home sales staff in Michigan. Upon reviewing the roster, I found they had a salesperson named Don who, whimsically, would paw the ground before a prospect arrived. "Is he about 6 feet tall with brown hair and a scar on the left side of his face?" I asked.

"Dead on," was the answer. "How do you know him?"

"Well, he worked for me for a year and a half in the Texas recreational land business and was one heck of a closer. How is he adjusting to new home sales?"

His sales manager said, "A bit rough. He steamrollers people too fast, but with some toning down I believe he can make the grade."

We spent considerable time working with Don's empathy until he became a believer and user. Some time later, I was informed that he had joined the ranks of master closers. By definition, the master closer can consistently bring to contract one out of ten registered prospects with a suitable balance of ego drive and empathy.

TOM TALKS... About Closing

Master closers understand that closing should be fun. That's why they close on the homesite or in the field model or home the prospects will buy. That's where excitement and buying fever mount to a crescendo. So, it's logical to close there. However, the journeyman salesperson doesn't do that. They think closing the sale is couched in numbers or magically will come out of the computer. Every master closer in our business agrees that the closing process should occur when and where ownership transfers. That's called the purchase target – or to put it another way – "The more you site, the more you write!"

Joe

Know Your Sales People

One of the greatest sales managers of all time was a gentleman named Joe Bertling who for many years managed the John Crosland Company in Charlotte, North Carolina. Crosland enjoyed a market share that often exceeded 40% of all the new homes sold in the area. To run that kind of sales operation with over fifty sales persons required extreme discipline and superb organization skills as well as a deep understanding of people.

Joe was the inventor of cross selling. He would allow a portion of his sales staff to cross sell or take a prospect from Community A into Community B if that better suited the prospect's requirements. It was done on a limited basis but was highly successful. In fact, we did a research study on the matter and determined that the cross selling captured from

15% to 20% more sales than would have normally been sold. Bertling put up with all kinds of flak for his cross selling operations from inside and outside the company, but stayed the course and made it the model for future cross selling operations.

The great point about Joe is he really knew his people. When you flew into Charlotte to conduct a training program, Joe would meet you at the airport. We'd repair to a coffee shop and review each salesperson. Joe developed the Strong Suit/Short Suit Worksheet where he would review the strengths and weakness of each salesperson with actions to be taken to correct those weaknesses. Every salesperson would be reviewed in great detail until we called it a night. Joe was the consummate reader of his sales people. He knew when they were going up or going down the motivation and production curve, when they were suffering from burn out, and when it was time to hold them or fold them. He was the ultimate sales manager of one of the housing industry's greatest sales teams.

The jist of this story is: Sales people must know their prospects and sales managers must know their sales people. Remember, as a sales manager, your customers are your sales people. Your job is to coach your people to heights of success they never dreamed possible. Salespersons should know themselves well enough so they can focus on bringing their short suits up to speed while embellishing their strengths or long suits.

Andrew Carnegie said it well, "Your competitor can match you in a thousand ways, but if your people are better, you have a priceless advantage." I say, "Companies don't compete. People compete."

HOW TO INSURE SUCCESS

The coun*sell*ing formula for excellence would not be complete without indexing these critical areas to insure success. **To be the best of the best, you must ...**

1. Set goals!
2. Don't put off till tomorrow what you can do today!
3. Exercise time management.
4. Acquire a selling process and be consistent.
5. Push the envelope of supreme discipline.
6. Take time to bond, and if possible, connect.
7. Discover the profile of your prospects.
8. Marry the prospect and product.
9. Neutralize objections with confidence.
10. Work to improve closing skills.
11. Organize a professional follow-up system – and then stick to it!
12. Service the buyers during and after the sale.
13. Utilize professional prospect sourcing.
14. Ask more questions and be a better listener!
15. Exercise focus and accountability.
16. Embrace boundless enthusiasm.
17. Learn how to sell and close with your financing.
18. Balance Ego and Empathy.
19. Build a career track through continuing education.
20. Evaluate yourself – Ruthlessly!

John

The Broker Co-op King

A southern company was blessed with a star salesperson named John who finished second in the national "Salesperson of the Year" awards program of the National Association of Home Builders (NAHB). That year he wrote and closed 148 sales! His sales manager said about half those sales came through his exceptional broker co-operation program.

"Just for fun," I said, "Why don't we try an experiment during our lunch hour? Let's ask John to take an hour and fifteen minute lunch break calling his team of brokers to see if any of them had a sale for the next thirty day time frame." John agreed. We asked him to make a list of all the brokers he called during the lunch break with any names, addresses, and phone numbers of possible buyers they would bring to John's job with the date and time of appointment. If any of these prospects became sales in the next thirty day time frame, John would earn a $500 bonus. He was thrilled about the challenge and went straight to his phone. He worked while we ate. After lunch, he tendered a list of a half-dozen names to his sales manager and guaranteed one of those names would be a broker/co-op sale. We showed it to the sales staff and they doubted any network could produce a sale on such short notice. Imagine our surprise when one of the designees came to contract the following weekend. John earned his $500 and proved to his staff that a network of ready, willing, and able real estate brokers was one of the new home salesperson's greatest assets – and an asset to the general brokerage community as well. General real estate brokers have what builder sales people need – new home prospects. And, new home sales people have what general brokers need – the availability of exciting new homes in new locations.

Broker cooperation is a wonderful institution properly executed and can cause the whole real estate community to thrive. And, don't forget the national economy. Every time a new home is sold there are 278 related goods and services that bring dollars into the public domain which heightens GDP. In this day and age, we need more government cooperation to fuel the housing industry, so we can write more sales of new homes which creates more jobs and fosters prosperity!

TOM TALKS... About Asking Questions

Intelligent questions allow you to:

1. **Identify** clearly the type prospect you are dealing with.
2. **Qualify** early in the selling process the "go" or "no-go" profile which can be an efficient time saver.
3. **Understand** the buyer's current situation such as agenda, hot button interests, and buying stage.
4. **Establish** the necessary rapport or comfort level that is vital for effective communications.
5. **Determine** the decision making process and who is instrumental in its process.
6. **Uncover** significant shortfalls or strong suits between you and the competition.
7. **Reinforce** credibility and breed confidence by demonstrating a concern for the prospects' well being.
8. **Encourage** a rock solid information flow based on plain and honest dealings.
9. **Position** yourself above and beyond the competition.
10. **Discover** the buyer's hidden checklist for purchase.

"You will be paid more money for asking the right questions than for knowing the right answers."

~Tom Richey

Earline

At the Top and Still Learning

The old Del Webb Corporation was building and marketing the mature lifestyle in its Sun Citys and had some of the finest sales staffs ever. They did not spare the horses hiring top flight personnel and training with proven practices and procedures. The sales staff was organized within the best tenets of sales management. Generally, for a major community there was a vice president of sales and marketing, a sales manager, and under the sales manager there may have been one to three floor sales managers. Was this overkill? Not in the results! When Del Webb opened Sun City, Las Vegas, extensive research said to staff with five sales people, since Las Vegas would not be a major market for mature lifestyle buyers. Boy, were they wrong! At the end of the day, Sun City, Las Vegas was staffed with twenty full time salespersons and everyone made money.

One day prior to Grand Opening, we were standing in front of a line of twelve model homes with the sales staff front and center. I commented we would initiate our F.A.S.T. system of sales training (Flashcard Assisted Sales Training). This meant each salesperson would write a set of flashcards for each room in each model. On average, there would be ten to twelve flashcards per model home. Let's take Model One. The first flashcard would be entitled, "Exterior." The front would recite the features and the back would be the benefits of each feature. So, the card was a feature/benefit card on one part of the model. The next flashcard would address the foyer with the features on the front, benefits on the back. The next flashcard would be the living room. Features on the front, benefits on the back and so on until every room including the garage was detailed out in flashcards. Then the salesperson would write up the next model until all twelve models were completed. Why not have those cards prepared in advance? The learning was in the doing and cross pollination of ideas since every salesperson had a different perspective.

The Del Webb sales staffs were highly trained and motivated. They enjoyed a challenge. However, on this day when we mentioned that every salesperson had to prepare a series of flashcards on all twelve models, a groan came from the group.

"Holy smokes!" one salesperson blurted. "You expect us to pull over 100 flashcards on twelve different model homes?"

I was rescued by Del Webb's number one nationally recognized salesperson, a lady named Earline. She stepped forward and said, "Every time I do these learning programs, it helps me immensely with the customers. If I can do it, I don't see why you can't do it."

That was a trainer's dream, having a star performer step up and endorse the material and the method. As expected, Earline went on to peak sales at this community.

Another Del Webb vignette: One of the eastern communities sported sixteen different models dressed to the nines. Every model was decorated to the hilt, often with lavish ideas that far exceeded the average buyer's budget. For example, $50,000 kitchens, $25,000 wine rooms, $15,000 cigar vaults, and the kitchen appliance packages drop-shipped from Europe! Del Webb was a master at painting dreams and sowing the seeds of discontent. This kind of merchandising sold a ton of homes. However, it put a burden on the salesperson to explain the disparity between "what you see is what you get" and the blown out "house of ideas." One day a salesperson raised a particularly knotty challenge.

"Mr. Richey, why do the decorators fill the models with things people can't afford, don't want, or can't have?"

The thought struck me that it was not what they see or what you say, but how you say it. Instead of talking about all the decorator features in a particular model, why not have an answer to the buyer's often unstated question, "Why so much extravagance?" The answer was, "Welcome to the world's largest model home park. Only a company the size of Del Webb could bring you such an event. Here's how you enjoy it. When you go through each model home, remember that each model is a **living catalog** of what you could design and build in your home. Sure, most of what you see you may not want, but if there is something there that's in your budget, like a wine cooler, the living catalog will show you how it would look in your home. I think you'll agree this is more compelling than looking at it on a printed page, wouldn't you agree?" The buyers' eyes would light up since they now understood why there were so many mind boggling extras in a model home – not to confuse but to clarify.

There was also a plethora of master marketing ideas within the Webb organization. I was sitting in a waiting room in Sun City, Tucson and I saw a giant hand-tooled, leather scrapbook that beckoned one to open its cover. The first page was a photograph of President Richard Nixon with a letter from him thanking the Del Webb organization for sending him a Golden Crown. The crown represented the Best Builder Award for Mature Buyers in the state of Arizona. Turning to page two, we saw the governor of Arizona congratulating the company on winning the Golden Crown. Turning to page three there was the governor of California congratulating the company. The album contained page after page of congratulations until I reached my letter at the very back of the book congratulating the company on winning the Golden Crown. Years later, after the original company was acquired by Pulte, I was told they had bestowed that award upon themselves and had sent out the Golden Crowns to the various celebrities knowing they would receive congratulatory letters. What great fodder for a spectacular endorsement book which tempted you to open its pages in the waiting area. How many people saw the endorsement by the President of the United States and thought this was great stuff. Whether you agree or disagree with the methodology, strive for as much quality recognition as you can and merchandise it to the hilt. It pays off.

Del Webb did a lot of things right. In several communities, the sales people were required to memorize the romantic names of the different finishes such as floor tiles, vinyl resilient, wood floors, granite and marble countertops, cabinetry colors, paint and roofing. In other words, you had to know the nomenclature of the colors and textures and be able to weave them into a presentation. "This is our 16 inch burnt sienna Tuscany tile laid on the bias." Or, "Our midnight black, hardwood mahogany floor with a polyurethane surface to ward off nicks and scratches." Or, "How about our granite countertop resplendent in burnt umber earth tones." Having a vocabulary of exotic names for the finishes gave the sales professional a differentiation the others did not have.

Medal point: When so many homes and products look the same, the sales people and the homes that are differentiated will win the battle for the contract.

Del Webb was also a fan of ladders which ranked a salesperson according to proficiency. In any one of the Del Webb salesperson's bullpens, or salesperson staging areas, you would see a ladder with the No. 1 ranked salesperson at the top and the lowest ranked person at the bottom. But wait; was the recognition for sales written? No. The ladder reflected ten measurements of a salesperson's worthiness. They were 1) Follow up, 2) Realtor base, 3) Product knowledge, 4) Counselling & closing skills, 5) negotiating skills, 6) Offsite marketing, 7) Process management, 8) Sales goals, 9) Desire, and 10) Team player.

TOM TALKS... About the Value of Time

How much is a salesperson's time worth? That is an interesting question from which you will get different answers. Let's start with how much time it takes to bring a sale to completion. Back in the salad selling days of 2004 to 2006, the sales came quickly. People were lining up to take advantage of the real estate boom and it didn't take a great deal of time to put people into contract. Although there have been sales people who said from the time you meet a customer at the front door until completion with all the coordination, communication, and grunt work in between, it could well be a four to six hour time frame. Today, we believe the time frame has expanded considerably. We call it the Extended Buying Cycle or EBC. People are now taking longer to come to a decision. Six to eight months may not be unusual and two to three years in the mature lifestyle sector may be the norm. So, what does this mean? Three events must be in place: 1) Qualify and discover the buyer's desires fast, 2) Move the sale forward by focusing on those product desires and housing design while demonstrating true value for true price, and 3) Probe for and establish one-of-a-kind and come to closure by asking for the order.

Sales people, today, have suggested that when they are touring prospects toward a one-of-a-kind and a close on site, their time could be worth as much as $1,000 an hour. When they are soft multiple closing prospects on site or back in the sales center, their worth per hour could be $500 to $750. When they are making an initial presentation with a new prospect family, their time could be worth between $200-$300 an hour. When making follow up phone calls it could be $75 to $125 an hour. And, of course, when sitting in a sales center reading a novel or watching a mini-TV (which is a No-No), the salesperson's time is worth zero!

If a sales professional's time is most highly prized when they are touring customers, then why doesn't the salesperson do more of this? In other words, why not set more on site appointments for off traffic times? Why not find ways to extend the presentation with the first or second time visitor? Why not find time to do a more professional, in-depth, budget-oriented financing presentation to give the customers a one-of-a-kind in the financing arena that dovetails with their one-of-a-kind in the housing area? In other words, take a page from the retailer. The reason supermarkets expanded into ethical drugs, household goods, clothing, insurances, and a wide variety of products is that once a viable buyer is in the store, why not give that buyer more time to purchase more product and book more profit? That is why we subscribe to the blanket community presentation from the front entry all the way in. We suggest finding several impact stations and driving customers to those views, vistas, or model exteriors at the end of cul-de-sacs. That's why we believe in alternate financing presentations, or an old fashioned walk through of the benefits of the builder's construction. We need to remember that 25% of all buyers looking at model homes are left brainers who must know how a home is constructed or they are down the road finding a salesperson who can tell them this. In today's world, sales people have to be more knowledgeable and skilled than in days of yore.

So, take a weekly checklist and determine how and where you spend your time. If you are not investing enough time touring prospects, your income will suffer. Same if you are not in front of enough prospects in the closing zone or making enough follow up phone calls.

Think now, what is your time worth?

TOM TALKS... About Being Clear, Concise, Complete

It's a shame so many salespeople use language that confuses buyers. An example of dis-communication: "I know you understand what you think I said, but I'm not sure you realize that what you heard is not what I meant."

Clarify and clean up your language and watch your sales soar.

Dave

Rankings: Fact or Fancy?

In any discussion of ranking sales professionals, the thought surfaces that in some cases the job makes the salesperson. Historically, a fast selling job would create sales volumes that were not necessarily earned. Or conversely, a slow selling job might require immense sales power to work out of it. So rankings can be irrelevant. Personally, I like sales people to know where they stand against their own goals and the company goals. Some of the most productive information for ranking ladders are developed by one's own sales staff. Accordingly, it is not management mandating what constitutes professional selling standards, it is the sales staff. They develop an MPS – a **M**inimum to **M**edian to **M**aximum **P**erformance **S**tandard which becomes the foundation of their presentation. In the selling or counselling process, they work hard not to depart from their MPS.

Years ago, I met a fascinating individual in the Kansas City Chiefs locker room after a football game. His name was Dave and he had just retired as commander of the Forestal aircraft carrier, one of the largest atomic powered carriers in existence. Dave was impressed by the fact that all the coaches had ladders in their offices rating the players they were coaching. He offered he also had a ladder on the aircraft carrier rating the pilots. However, as Dave put it, "This ladder was a great deal more serious than a football team's ladder or a salesperson's ladder, because the pilots were measured by skills and safety. The safest pilots were at the top and the most dangerous were at the bottom. If you were the bottom three to four pilots, you had the real possibility of flying off the flight deck and killing yourself."

If rankings are serious stuff in the military and in the high paid world of pro football, why wouldn't they be used in sales and sales management? Why wouldn't sales people rank themselves personally on their best selling attributes with the understanding the bottom three to four would bring themselves up to speed immediately? Why wouldn't sales managers be more proactive grouping their sales staff into top third, middle third, and bottom third? The challenge is to cause the bottom third of your staff to be better than the competition's top third. Makes sense, doesn't it?

Simon

Using Financing to Close the Deal

The mature lifestyle market is a very patient buyer. To come to closure quickly the sales professional had better have all the facts or access to the facts. Working at a Shea Homes community in Northern California, I had the pleasure of talking to a husband and wife who had purchased a home that morning. Over lunch, the couple commented that several years before they had come to the same community with the idea of buying a home. They loved the lifestyle, the location, the ambiance, the amenities, the possibility of making new friends, and all the wonderful nuances that come with mature lifestyle living. However, when the salesperson asked how they planned to pay for the home and the couple said cash, the husband admitted when he put his pen onto the check to sign off for several hundred thousand dollars, he just couldn't do it.

"Letting loose of that much cash at that point in my life was a God-fearing event and one we just couldn't manage. This morning," the gentleman continued, "when it came time to write a check for a similar home that was now more expensive, once again I balked at writing a check for cash until Simon, the sales counselor, suggested a financing program. I didn't know much about financing, but he explained it well."

The purchaser went on that when he learned the benefit of leverage when purchasing a home at his age, he went on to sign the agreement with alacrity. What the salesperson clarified was rather than tie up $400,000 of cash, why not use a small part of that for the initial investment and put the rest into an interest bearing account. With a reasonable return, that account could help pay for part of the debt service. However, the debt service, because of the front end interest load, could create a tax write off which could help defray the federal taxes on this couple's stocks and bonds. In the long run the children should be happy, because while real estate values are volatile now, real estate has grown in value over the historical peaks and valleys. Today, you buy a home for the lifestyle, pride of ownership, ambiance, and the good life. Tomorrow, if there happens to be a gain in value, count your blessings, but "protect your money by leveraging your money," was the salesperson's message. The family bought the message, OKed the agreement, and everybody was happy. Every time a home is sold, research shows there are multitudes of related goods and services that buoy the nation's economy. So, you sales practitioners ... Sell more homes! That's right, selling homes creates jobs which bolsters the economy which makes our nation the best housed country in the world!

TOM TALKS... About A Trained Sales Staff

We had some major executives of Centex Homes in session, including the chairman of the board. We were discussing what makes sales people successful and we landed on the closing ethic. What a shame, we commiserated, that sales people across the United States don't stay in the closing game longer and ask more closing questions.

I presented the scenario, "What would happen if every Centex salesperson across the United States would close one more prospect out of a hundred families in the door, or in short, convert to one percent more efficiency?"

The chairman took out his pen and did some quick calculations. His answer was astounding, "Tom, if every salesperson in our system closed to a one percent greater efficiency, that would bring $33,000,000 of additional profit to the bottom line."

Several months later, I asked a major regional builder how much more profit a one percent increase in closing efficiency would bring his operation. The answer was a clean, clear $6,000,000. When additional sales are made without raising overhead, that's pure profit, and the company prospers, as does the sales professional! For the same energy, expertise, and time consumption, sales and marketing are working much more efficiently and profits to the bottom line can go sky high!

The housing industry has never really grasped this critical point. **The quickest way to book profits is to recruit a team of highly trained and motivated sales people.** The sites are developed, the houses are built, and the company is waiting for contracts to be written and profits booked. If a company has super professional expertise on its team, that company will make the sales other builders miss and that company will prosper. Let's say it again. In today's challenging market, the housing industry must learn that the surest way to book profits is to hire and develop a highly trained and motivated sales staff. It is as simple as that!

THE PROSPECT'S DILEMMA

"I don't know who you are."
"I don't know your company."
"I don't know the integrity of your company."
"I don't know your company's quality standards."
"I don't know your company's service policies."
"I don't know your company's track record."
"I don't know what kind of house you build."

"Now -- what in the world was it you wanted to sell me?"

Greg

The Selling Machine

Greg was a high energy salesperson who believed in self-prospecting. In fact, he had sold twenty-nine homes in twenty-nine days. If he sold thirty homes in thirty days and all sales funded, that would be a company record and was worthy of a bonus. I persuaded management to go overboard with a high recognition prize. Greg would be awarded $1,000 if he sold and closed thirty homes in thirty days, but only after all the sales were proven good. I was on pins and needles the final day hoping Greg would come through. What a great endorsement it would be to the forty-three person staff if he made this number. At this time, we were teaching the sales staff to go offsite to follow up and cinch the sale, not wait for it at the sales office door. Greg knew how to work offsite.

About mid-day, I called the community, curious to see what Greg was doing. Alas, he was not there. His partner confirmed Greg had not shown up for work. This was highly unusual for this master closer. He always reported for work and expended long hours prospecting with his phone. As the day was winding down I called again. No Greg. Now, I became concerned. Was he mugged? Hijacked? Taken ill? Suffered a heart attack? What in the world happened? At 2 a.m. in the morning, I got a phone call that woke me from a deep sleep. Lo and behold, it was Greg exclaiming he was in a rental apartment and had just wrapped up a new home contract. He sounded like the kid that raided the cookie jar when he asked sheepishly, "Mr. Tom, could we make this retroactive to last month's report?" I told him not to worry. "Thirty sales in thirty days, that's a Herculean task. Congratulations! Now, Greg," I asked, "be honest, why didn't you come to work?"

The answer was, "I'm so sorry, Mr. Tom, but I couldn't do that. I knew that if I came to the job and waited for a be-back sale, I was leaving my fate up to chance. So, I decided to go into the apartments of my best prospects until I found someone who had visited me before and who would buy now!"

He wrote the sale on an in-home follow-up with a be-back prospect. Certainly the sale would not have happened had he waited for it. Whereas, he bent company policy for leaving the job, we rewarded him for writing thirty sales in thirty days.

This example has several **medal points**. First of all, a producing salesperson may have to bend the rules once in a while. If they are bent too much, they have to be chastised. Discipline is critical to operating a well knit sales staff. However, he did notify his partner telling him he was going all out to make the sale. The bottom line was he produced, and how he produced! The sales manager has to make up his or her mind whether this departure from the playbook is acceptable.

The second **medal point** is this master closer knew that if you must have a sale, it is far better to make it happen than wait for it to happen. How many sales people wait for be-backs that never come? On the other hand, how many sales people find out where those possible buyers are and go A.F.S., Away From the Site, where the business is?

Greg was a master at following up prospects and closing them when they were closable.

TOM TALKS... About Thinking Outside the Box

A canning company was trying to sell white salmon and having difficulty breaking into the market because of the popularity of pink salmon. Finally, they came up with a selling solution. On the label of every can they printed ... "This salmon guaranteed not to turn pink in the can."

Bob

Proper Balance Produces Lasting Sales

Bob was a sales prodigy. I recruited him from the entertainment industry where he had made $50,000 a year selling for Decca Records. That was a lot of money in 1963. Bob came into the housing industry with high ego. Surely he could earn a ton of money with the high commissions we were paying compared to what he was making selling records. Trouble was, Bob's ego was often out of control. He was so cocky that the personality trait alienated buyers. It even isolated him from his selling partners; so much so, I had a hard time keeping him on the job. Bob was a classic case of all ego drive and no empathy. Yet, he was a master closer and wrote a lot of business. Unfortunately, with ego driven salespersons, it also brings high cancellations. Ego has no place in sales unless it is harmoniously balanced with empathy. We go for the close with ego. We back off or adjust to the customer's feelings with empathy. We move forward with more ego; we adjust with empathy. It's like baking a cake; a pinch of this and a dash of that. There has to be balance. Bob had no balance. He was off the chart with ego drive.

One day I was driving out to the community to terminate him and he pleaded so hard to keep his job that I finally said, "Bob, I'll give you one more chance and one only. If you don't dial down this bombastic, bloated ego of yours, you'll never make it in sales." Let's give Bob a kudo. He listened intently and said, "Boss, I want this job so badly I'll do whatever you tell me."

Whereupon I countered, "Whenever you feel like blowing off steam, intimidating people, or pushing buyers against their will, take a deep breath and ask yourself if you really want to lose this commission." That's all it took! Bob became one of the top producers in Southern California for many years and was a credit to every sales staff he worked for.

Medal Point: Unbridled ego is crippling. Unfocused empathy is useless. Only the proper balance of ego and empathy will cause a salesperson to prosper.

"If you think education costs money, try ignorance!"
~Tom Richey

Steve

Down Home Professional Selling

Steve was a selling machine in a Bull Durham disguise. One day I was driving north of Houston to find a recreation property. No one knew where it was until I entered a modular sales office planted on four concrete blocks. The sign said "Country property for sale. See the expert, Steve." As I opened the screened enclosure, there was Steve sitting behind a makeshift desk watching a baseball game on TV. He had on the traditional Levi 509 jeans, boots, a cowboy shirt with pearl buttons, and a wide brimmed straw hat. Steve was doing the salesperson's no-no – rolling a cigarette from his Bull Durham pouch.

"Hi, my name is Tom Richey."

Steve countered with "Steve, broker for the best properties in the area. What are you looking for?"

"Well, Steve, I'm just looking for directions to a recreational area. Let me show you my map. I'm lost."

"Most people are lost when they come in here," Steve countered. "Let's see if I can help you. Well, the job is about five miles up the road and it will take you a few minutes to get there. By the way, would you like a nice cold drink? It's hot outside."

I said, "It might be kind of nice." So we began to jaw a bit. At this point, Steve pulled out a big plat map and said, "Just got a listing on the most gorgeous country property you'll ever see. It's 100 acres of land, right in the path of progress with a five acre lake, next to a national park and two sides of paved county road. Property like that doesn't come around very often. Furthermore, it is the highest elevation in Walker County and has a stand of tall pine trees on it. Why don't we go look at it?"

"Sorry, Steve. I don't have the time. I've got to get up and scout out this recreation property. Perhaps another day."

As I got up to leave, he got up too and followed me to the door.

"Tell you what. You must be in real estate, right?"

"You got that right," I said.

"What kind of property are you looking for?" he asked.

"Well, I'm not really looking for property." I said, "I'm looking to sell for a landowner. I've got a pretty good sales staff that can do things like this."

He pressed on. "Being a real estate man, you gotta take a few minutes and see this piece of land. I'll bet you've never seen a spread like it anywhere in this neck of the woods. Come on, let's go in my truck?"

"Sorry Steve, I'm really short on time."

"No, a good real estate man always has his nose out for a knock out property. I'm not asking you to buy it. Maybe you can co-broke a sale with me. Come on, let's go."

Now, there was just something about old Steve, the country boy that you just couldn't resist. Perhaps it was his down home friendliness and subtle persistence, or maybe he just looked the part of a country salesman. Anyway, he was going to get you in his truck and take you to that property and that was that!

Sure enough, we turned off the main North/South freeway from Houston to Dallas and drove a short way down the paved country road until the entrance to the property appeared. It was everything Steve said it was – over 100 acres of gently rolling terrain with a stand of trees on a high piece of ground and a sky blue lake. It was a dream property dressed up and ready for a hunting lodge.

"Come on," Steve said, "Let's walk down to the lake and throw a line in the water."

I said, "Steve, I really can't spare the time."

He said, "Of course you can. Let's enjoy the better things of life for a minute. Gotta smell the roses once in a while. Tell you what; wouldn't you like to own property like this?"

I said, "Frankly, I haven't thought about it."

Steve said, "It might be just the right time to think about it because the minute I advertise it, it's sold. Flat sold. I've never seen a property like this anywhere in my eighteen years experience up here."

Steve was beginning to sow the seed of discontent. Now he launched a most unusual close.

"Tell you what," he said, "Let's throw a line in the water. If you or I catch a bass within fifteen minutes, you buy the property. If not, I buy you lunch. How does that sound?"

I was getting quite hungry by that time and thought it would be a great way to get a free lunch so, why not? Now, Steve must have had those fish trained because within seven to eight minutes there was a giant jerk on his line and Steve was reeling in a beautiful bass, true to his word. Now the onus was on me. I had agreed to buy the property if Steve caught a fish. So, after a further tour of the property and a quick resolution in my mind anchored by a "Why not?" I was back in Steve's office writing a contract.

I said goodbye to Steve and proceeded to find my recreation project. When I got home, my wife raked me over the coals. "You're supposed to be a knowledgeable real estate pro and you advise people not to buy property unless they thoroughly check it out. Here you buy property without knowing anything about it. You probably paid too much!"

So my well meaning spouse persuaded me to go to the bank the very next morning to stop order the check. Unfortunately, I was delayed and did not arrive at the bank until twenty-five minutes after ten. Steve Wilson, the country bumpkin broker, had arrived at 9:00 a.m. sharp and had cashed the check. So, the sale was a done deal and I owned 100 acres.

Let's fast forward twenty-seven years. That piece of property is still in my name. Progress has grown up all around it. There are countless pleadings to sell. And, despite the demise of real estate, the value has held very well. Kudos go to the country salesperson, Steve Wilson, who with the power of assumption, positive mental attitude, and a little bit of chutzpah with that trained fish, persuaded me, the "real estate professional" to buy unresearched property. There are sales people in this world who can sell tennis balls to golfers and that's what makes our economy hum. We are a nation of marketers and merchandisers. I say, God bless the Steve Wilsons of the world. At this point in the history of our nation, we need a lot more of them.

Linda

Getting the Name is Critical

We were moving along fast in the training sessions and the salespersons were gathered around the topo table in a mature lifestyle development in New Jersey. We had the hostess handling traffic at the front door. A diminutive couple comes in and I heard the husband say, "We will absolutely and most certainly not register with you. We are sick and tired of being on lists and having people call us. If we like what we see here, we'll tell you." So, the hostess proceeded to direct them toward the model homes and ceased the request for the name, address, and phone number. Now, we in sales know that if you don't get the contact information, you are out of business with that prospect family. While it is grand opening day for the customers when they arrive in the sales center, it is grand closing day if the salesperson does not get follow-up data. Fortunately, this hostess was saved by the bell when the couple returned and the elderly gentleman said, "Gertrude and I really love this place. Now, I would like to give you our name, address, and phone number. You can even have a salesperson call us if they want to." Buyers giving contact information after a model tour is not unusual. Saying they like it so much they want a salesperson to call is extraordinary. That is the power of merchandising. We quickly dispersed a salesperson from the training group so she could introduce herself to the family and establish a bond. The point here is all too many sales people say, "Brochures on the table, model that way. Come back and I'll answer your questions." They do so without getting a name, address, and phone number so follow up is a non event. For sure, the occupational hazard of selling new and resale homes throughout our country is the directive, "Pick up the brochure on the table, check out the model home, and then I'll be more than happy to answer your questions."

For years I thought this was endemic only to the United States. Surely other countries of the world would not sell the same way. Knowing that by survey 50% of all presentations in our country are styled in this manner, I wanted to test my theory that it was unique only to the United States. What a surprise when I entered a sizeable development in Tel Aviv and a salesperson in broken English said, "Brochure on table, model that way." Or, in a recent foray into Oman where I was stunned by the beauty of a seaside development, I found the same occupational hazard.

The salesperson, while sitting down, bellowed, "Pick up brochure on table, go that way, and turn left to model."

Let's go to Poland. We were driving from Warsaw to Cracow when we encountered a new home community with a Grand Opening in full swing. We decided to act like potential buyers and go through their process. We experienced five – yes, five – different contacts during the Grand Opening presentation. The first contact violated all the rules. The hostess blurted out, "Brochure on table, model that way." No. 2 was a tour guide of the sales office. No. 3 handoff was a model demonstrator. No. 4 was a tour guide to the inventory and No. 5 was the contract writer who appeared to be untrained, unconfident, and said, "Contract on table, pick up, read, I come back, you sign." Interesting that she was speaking English, although we had feigned to be Polish. This was not a pleasurable home buying experience. Telling someone to pick up a brochure is simply directing them to take home a brochure where nineteen times out of twenty nothing happens. Brochures are used to reinforce information and data, and are occasionally used as a hand off tool to a friend. They do not drive sales nor are they intended to. Better a salesperson say to the customer, "Here at Richbuilt Homes we do things a little differently. Let me ask you a few questions, find out what's important to you, and then see how close we can come to building your dream home. Wow, based on what you shared with me, let's see if this floor plan fits the bill." Then we give the brochure.

Judy

The Old Schmo vs. the Young Pro

One thing about mystery shopping; the tale of the tape doesn't lie. We were asked to shop a community by a major homebuilder north of Houston, Texas. It was a large complex community with a lot of recreational pull. We figured it would require one of our best husband/wife shopping teams. So up north they went to shop a tenured but reportedly burned out salesperson. In the briefing, I was told he had over ten years selling experience. Here's what happened. Our shoppers walked in the door and were promptly greeted by a, "Come in here to buy a home?"

My shoppers said, "Don't know. What have you got?" (On the shopper's summary, we were told the salesperson had his feet planted firmly on the desk and as the conversation developed the feet never came down.)

Salesperson countered with, "You don't want to buy a home here. I haven't sold a home here in three months."

Our shoppers said, "Well, we heard this Woodlands area was a great place to live. What's wrong?"

"Aw shucks," said the salesman. "If I had any money I'd drive up north a bit and buy at that Kingwood place. They've got great homes there."

My shoppers continued their assignment, did due diligence and self-toured three model homes. Usually on a shopping visit when there is no other traffic in sight, the salesperson will enter a model at some time and try to engage. Not so here. He never appeared. It was all on the tape. Returning from the model tour and upon entering the sales office, the salesperson (with feet still on the desk) shouted, "What did you think?"

The shoppers answered, "We liked the second model."

"That dog?" admonished the salesperson. "No way you can like that. We've never sold one of those!"

Keep in mind that mystery shoppers or professional evaluators are trained to coax or cajole some information out of the salesperson. Hopefully it will be positive, but if not, so be it. The tape didn't lie! When they probed the salesperson further, he shut down and said, "I've told management what to build but they don't listen to me!" He never ingratiated. He never questioned their reason for the visit. He never presented an acceptable demeanor, and he never proffered one bit of positive information. Let's note here there have been so called marketing gurus who have actually said at educational programs that a highly trained and motivated salesperson doesn't make a sizable difference at the end of the day. Don't you believe it! How would you like to have this turkey representing your homes? This presentation ranks numero uno in my sales agents' Hall of Shame.

When my shoppers were blown out on a shopping assignment, they were directed to shop the nearest community to see if there was an epidemic of negativity in the area. They would shop the closest community with the most comparable homes. The shopping unit walked right across the street and entered the competing builder's office which happened to be Pulte Homes. The sales lady was up front and center greeting my shoppers with enthusiasm. "Welcome to my community. My name is Judy, and yours is?"

"Thank you so much for visiting Pulte Homes in the Woodlands. Let's sit down and discuss your new home needs." She asked several questions that gave insight into the buyers' requirements and then said, "I can't sell you property today because I'm sales ahead of construction. In fact, I won't have a new release for about six weeks. Seems like you're in the market for a new home, am I correct?"

The shoppers answered, "If we find the right one."

The sales lady countered, "Great! Tell you what, let's go look at the new property I'll have available in six weeks."

My shoppers reared back and said they'd just like a brochure, probably because they weren't being paid a dime extra for this shop. The Sales Pro persisted.

"I've got such a gorgeous property you just have to see it. Come on. Let's go in my car."

With the fine art of assumptive persuasion, she moved the shoppers into her vehicle and soon they were waltzing all over the rocks and rills in the dead heat of summer. You could hear my shoppers panting on the tape. You could sense her enthusiasm as she went from one homesite to another. Then she landed on a one-of-a-kind site that carried all the beauties of Texas property – tall trees, rich dark dirt, a level building site, and a view to a scenic pond. She built urgency by insisting that this property would sell fast once it came to market, but she couldn't sell it now because she didn't have the prices.

Back in the sales center, she booked an appointment for my shoppers to come back in six weeks. Now, get this! They returned to see the property six weeks later and bought a real honest to goodness home from this diminutive master closer.

Here, we have the real world comparison between a producing salesperson and a fly on the wall; a salesperson with **add**itude who adds profit to the bottom line versus a profit seeper. The two builders had similar products similarly priced. The other salesperson had caused her company to shine in the eyes of potential customers and was sales ahead of construction. Remember, the products were similar and they were fifty yards from each other. Examples like this are rampant, particularly in the world of mystery shopping. Again, we ask the question, "Who do you want selling for you? Salesperson A or Salesperson B?" That is the challenge of all salespersons – to practice, drill, and rehearse until they become masters at their chosen profession.

TOM TALKS... About Details

A top professional shared with me that one secret of her exterior demonstration "sell" was knowledge of how to explain roof pitch. Simply said, roof pitch is **rise** over **run**. The run or the horizontal is always in units of twelve. We refer to the rise first in relation to the run. For example, if the roof pitch rises six units on the rise and runs twelve units on the horizontal, which is a constant, it is a 6-12 roof pitch. If it rises seven units vertically and runs the constant of 12 units on the horizontal, it is a 7-12 roof pitch. A 12-12 roof pitch would be twelve units on the rise and twelve units on the run. You anchor this with a U-benefit by saying, "When real estate appraisers put a value on a home, they very often provide higher value for a higher roof pitch."

Debbie vs. Christy

Which Would You Hire?

For sure, the Untied States is the Mecca for model home merchandising. No country does it better. But as I assess the new home selling scene, I see a lack of focus and accountability on the sales side of the marketing equation. From my perspective, home builders are losing millions of dollars annually because of poor sales representation.

Some of this might be justified with the acknowledgement that in a white hot seller's market, who has to sell? But, in a black, cold, brutal housing market, you <u>have</u> to sell. In good times or bad, when you stop selling, profits go south and skills atrophy. This is precisely what has happened to the housing market.

Let's look at Christy from California as an example. In a recent on-site sales training session, Christy arrived late with a demeanor that said, "You can't teach me anything new." In fact, she announced in front of the team that since it was her day off, she'd be leaving after lunch.

We kicked off the training session with a call for preparation – the vital necessity of being organized to sell. When we outlined the need for a Visualizer presentation book – the sales office in a book – Christy said, "I don't need that. My buyers already know the floor plan they want and understand the dynamics of the market, because that's all on our community website."

We moved on to the need for a toolbox. In this scenario, we profiled a world class homesite demonstration consistently executed by a Midwest sales professional named Debbie. In this venue, she precedes the demo with a drive through the neighborhood. Her buyers are oriented to the site with a mounted community map, properly oriented to their location on the tour. At appropriate times, Debbie stops her vehicle and asks her prospective home buyers to walk to the dramatic overlook, or the scenic pond, or the cul-de-sac street scene with mix and match architecture. Every step of the way, Debbie is anchoring the presentation with a trial close or tie down. "Pretty view, isn't it?" "Wonderful spot to picnic with the kids, don't you think?" "Great ambiance, huh?" By the time they arrive at the homesite, these prospects are thoroughly sold on the community and they've grown accustomed to answering "yes" to Debbie's casual, yet well-planned questions.

At the property she will sell, Debbie parks her car across the street so the homesite looks larger as the prospects walk toward it. She opens the trunk of her car and offers ice cold water bottles from an ice chest. Then, she pulls out a large tub of selling materials she calls her tool box. Debbie winks to her buyers with provocation, "Now the fun starts."

Her first exercise places the wife on the right front with a red plastic cone, the husband on the left front with a cone. Now she walks diagonally across the site to create more visual space as she positions herself at the right rear with a cone. Next, she places a cone on the left rear corner. Then she jogs to her buyers and asks them to hold a measuring tape at the numbers end of the tape. "When the number hits 30 feet, that's our front set back line," she explains. She does the same with the side setback numbers and then places four more red cones on the building pad's corners. With eight Day-Glo red cones at the site's impact points, the property comes alive!

Now Debbie says, "Gorgeous building site isn't it? Can't you picture your new home built right here?" And she snaps a digital picture of the couple in the center of the pad. When asked about energy efficiency, she produces a compass to confirm the passive solar energy efficiency benefit.

Next, she gives an enlarged mounted floor plan to her buyers and asks them to orient it to the site. Now, Debbie takes a Magic Marker and points out the home's cross ventilation, access to the backyard, appropriate zoning of the plan and how it compliments the site. She finally closes with, "Perfect plan for this glorious homesite, isn't it?"

Now the series of exercises continues:

1) She flips the mounted plan over and asks her buyers to select an exterior which they can do because they are early in the phase.

2) She walks her home buyers to the rear property line where the homesite looks one-third larger when looking from the rear toward the front.

3) She takes a Ziploc bag out of her pocket, reaches down to the ground and selects several "special" rocks and a handful of dirt which she puts in the bag with her business card and says, "We'll staple this to your agreement so you'll have a souvenir of this special day."

4) Next she goes for the close with a gentle, "Have you found your one-of-a-kind? Great ... let's make it yours, shall we?" When the buyers balk, she reaches into her aluminum clipboard box to produce a new article where the Fed chairman is quoted as saying rates are on the rise.

5) After three soft multiple closes, she secures the agreement. At this landmark moment, she brings forth a Polaroid camera and takes three pictures of them putting up a sold sign. One is for the family, and two are for friends or possible referrals.

6) She leaves the eight cones on the site, since she knows buyers return to the property after executing the paperwork and she wants it to look compelling.

7) And, if her buyers had not purchased from her that day, she would have e-mailed them a visual record of the tour from her digital camera.

At this point in my sales training by example, Christy shouts out, "That's the dumbest thing I've ever heard! Why would anyone in their right mind waste all that time with those silly exercises? I never take anyone to the building site because too many negative things can happen out there?"

But wait, it gets worse!

When I revealed that the three biggest shortfalls in a new home salesperson's knowledge toolbox are lack of financing skills, lack of construction information, and lack of style and design familiarity, Christy blurted out, "I've never, ever gotten into financing. I just hand my lender's business card to the prospects and tell them to go find out how much home they can buy. And I never talk about construction or 'style and design,' whatever that is. But none of that has hurt my sales."

When I took the class deeper into the financing presentation with emphasis on the federal tax write-offs, Christy vehemently argued that, "there is <u>no</u> federal property tax deduction!"

After lunch, Christy left the training session in a huff saying, as she had predicted, that she hadn't learned anything new. Incidentally, Debbie is a world class sales pro who has been number one on a large sales staff for the past six years. Toolboxes like the one Debbie has are being used in tough, competitive markets nationwide. And it is also important to note that between 50 and 60 percent of today's selling is the utilization of financing. "It's not the price of the home that matters," the new home sales pro says, "It's how much home you can own for how little a month."

Now, here's the point. Unfortunately, the U.S. scene is rampant with sales people just like Christy. There are too many salespeople who started in the good times when very few had to sell. Frankly, there are too many salespeople representing builders with Christy's attitude of "You can't teach anything new."

When looking to hire a salesperson, I look for three things: a positive mental attitude, strong work ethic, and trainability. To have anything less representing the entire U.S. housing industry is a travesty.

As the market becomes increasingly difficult, home builders must ask themselves, "Am I better off with a world class product and marginal sales representation, or a marginal product and world class sales representation. The answer is obvious! However, the ultimate answer is why not have <u>both</u>! When it comes to the optimum in profit generation, you must have both.

Now, just imagine what you might achieve with both world class product and world class sales representation!

Analyze your sales staff today and take the necessary steps to immediately terminate the negative, divisive, lazy, unmanageable and/or untrainable salespeople who may be draining off your precious profit.

TOM TALKS... About Competition

Seems people are often concerned with the competition copying their presentations, or they feel they need to hold back contributions during training sessions. Recently, one sales crew said, "We have competition within our own company. We really don't want to share information with the rest of our team."

Sales professionals should understand that the competition is NOT another job within the company structure and not even the builder marketing a competing community. It's not even a resale home! The real competition is the home the family is in now. Does the new home and the salesmanship of it create burning desire? Does the buying public comprehend the real urgency – the fear of loss should it be sold to another family -- or the loss of loan qualification should rates rise?

Perhaps it's time to heed the advice of Rudyard Kipling, "They copied all they could follow and they tried to copy my mind, and I left them sweating and stealing and a year and a half behind!"

Joe, Bob, & Pete

What a Difference a Closer Makes

I never recruited harder in my life. When we opened Sky Harbour East, the nation's first high rise condominium, two sales people were hired. Bob was a master closer who had worked with me before. I knew he could sell and close. I scoured Florida far and wide to find a second salesperson. On the basis of glowing references which were checked diligently, I hired a second salesperson named Joe. After three months of pre-selling and launch, we sold just twenty-one residences. Selling a highrise condominium in those days was no piece of cake. People didn't understand purchasing a legally described airspace in the sky and resisted the idea summarily. At the end of the three months Bob had sold eighteen and Joe had sold three. I found out to my dismay that the references on Joe were half truths. Joe could "sell," but he couldn't close. When I dug further, I found that when it came to closing sales, Joe had a designated turnover/takeover closer who would close the transactions for him. This was Joe's weakness, and it was a big one. He simply could not close! So, I hired a gentleman named Pete who partnered with Bob. Pete came in and blew the doors off. The building was sold out in an additional three and a half month's time frame – sold from artist renderings and floor plans on paper!

The lesson was learned – in the game of selling property which is not a game at all – you can hire two "Joes" and have six sales after three months, or hire two "Bobs" and have thirty-six sales after three months. There is no substitute for a crack closer. At twenty-one sales, I barely kept the contract. With thirty-six sales, we'd have been heroes. Fortunately, when Pete's closing skills kicked in, we became the wizards of this new thing called condominium ownership.

TOM TALKS... About What Makes a Salesperson Successful

Being Assertive: A salesperson who can hold firm in negotiations and lead a customer to conclusion through force of will wins. Persistence is the sidebar to this trait.

Being a Risk Taker: Great salespersons innovate and take risks. They are not afraid to take a moon shot and above all, do not fear rejection.

Story 17

Tom

Pre Judging Prospects Not Allowed.

It was ribbon cutting day, the grand opening launch of the nation's first highrise condominium, Sky Harbour East. The brass turned out in all its finery. Dignitaries arrived from Washington. The senator and governor of Florida were there. It was a signal event. Just minutes before the official ceremony, a man dressed in only a bathing suit ran into the sales office disrupting the presentation. "I want to buy the two penthouses … I want to buy the two penthouses … I want to buy the two penthouses," he shouted. I had a dapper sales manager named Bill Smith. He was six foot five with a finely twirled handlebar mustache. He looked every bit the best part of the South Florida celebrity set. Bill quickly eased this gentleman towards the exit and was pushing him out the door when I said, "Bill, let me take over here, you go back to the ceremony."

I never saw one part of the event because when this gentleman said he wanted to buy the two penthouses and asked if we would take a check, I thought he was the real deal. Was he?

In a nano second we were jogging over the building pad of the highrise, across a creek, through some saw-grass and then into the beachside patio of this stunning home right on the Atlantic Ocean. I thought I'd really been had. Surely the competition had created this disruption to cause one of the great days of my life to go south. To my surprise, the bathing suit guy, who actually looked like the gardener for the premises, appeared at the back door with a large, hand tooled leather checkbook. He asked how much we needed to reserve the two penthouses.

I replied, "$25,000 ought to do it. Make the check out to ___." I received the check and noted the name of A.C. Ketzer. I had heard of an executive named Ketzer who was on the board of General Development Co. What I did not know was that he was Chairman of the Board of Bordo Food Products from Chicago. Mr. Ketzer wanted the two condominiums for his top executives so they could visit him while he wintered in Florida. When I took the check back to Bill Smith, he became apoplectic.

"You mean that guy in the bathing suit with the sweat pouring off him was a real buyer?"

"Yes, Bill, a real buyer! You can't judge a buyer by what he's wearing or not wearing!"

Most new or resale home agents have had similar experiences and they are wonderful stories to tell. What we have to be on the guard for today are those buyers that look like they don't have a dime when they might surprise you by buying the whole project. You qualify and discover not through visual senses but through mental probes.

TOM TALKS...

Three times in my life I've had this happen. We were sitting in a restaurant with the full sales team and company principals. The waitress is doing a great job attending to our needs. We talk amongst ourselves and decide to ask her if she knows anyone who is looking for a new home. We ask. Guess what? We receive. In three memorable cases - Muncie, Indiana, Reading, Pennsylvania, and Colorado Springs, Colorado - we were blessed with the answer, "My husband and I are looking for a new home."

"Great, you are talking to the right people. Let's see when you can visit our community and we'll give you the cook's tour."

In all three cases, the waitress and husband visited the property and bought a home. Sales are all around you. All you have to do is get proactive and ask!

Rosa

A Legend in Her Own Time

There was a 66-year old salesperson selling high rise condominiums in South Florida who was known as the icon of high rise selling. We were in the mystery shopping business. I hoped I could shop her expertise and find out what made her great. The day came for the opportunity. Putting my best shoppers on the project, we had the agreement with the principal of any company that if the salesperson performed a world class presentation, we would cut our shopping fee back to the salesperson if the company matched that amount of money as a reward for work well done. This was agreed to.

My shoppers arrived and the lady greeted them in her off site sales center. It was a modular unit that she shared with construction. No big deal. However, the tape showed her salesmanship was the real deal! She rose when my shoppers entered, escorted them over to a couple of building displays and then insisted they sit down for overview and indoctrination loaded with ingratiating questions.

While drinking coffee, they explored the features and benefits of the building and then the lifestyle conveniences within walking distance. The presentation lasted over thirty minutes. An abundance of non threatening questions were asked which assured the shoppers they were working with a true professional. Now it was time to tour the building. She said, "Would you kindly help me take these canvas chairs over to my building, and since the trades have left, we will be able to get up high enough in the high rise to give you some idea of the view?"

Upon entry to the building she escorted her prospects to one of the highest floors. They took the canvas chairs out on the balcony where the sun was beginning to set over the horizon. In a graciously modulated tone, she pointed out the beauty of the ochre sun over the shimmering water, "the picturesque" location, special composite of the white sand beaches, the convenience of near by amenities including restaurants, churches, and shopping, and even the number of days per year one could sun bathe. It was a complete travelogue of great benefit to someone who did not know the area. Then the canvas chairs were moved into the living/dining area where the discussion was question-based. For example, who's the chef in the family? Do you entertain formally or informally? What special furniture or graphic arts would adorn this room? How often do you watch TV? What are your requirements for guest quarters? Any special antiques or family heirlooms? How often would they come to Florida or would this be a primary residence? What was their budget for this type of property? Had they ever lived in high rise before? Were there any influencers such as children or attorneys? How soon would they make the move? All these questions came while sitting in canvas chairs in a dry wall environment. Boy was she painting pictures while she remained in the process of gaining agreement through gentle probes!

Then the chairs were moved into the owner's suite which was quite spacious and also had a view to the water. Again, the shoppers were asked to step onto the spacious balcony and relax in the canvas chairs while drinking in the view. The chairs were brought back in again to be placed on the living room balcony one more time. Now the sun was dipping into the horizon. The afterglow of the sunset illuminated the room and our icon of icons initiated the close. After some mind numbing word pictures, here came her call to action.

"Since I sense you love it so much, let's go ahead and make this one yours, shall we?"

The sale was wrapped up, but the presentation was not finished. She had a box type clipboard where she filled out the necessary paperwork while sitting in this emotional scene so there would be no buyer's remorse later. Then it was back to the sales center with canvas chairs in tow. Once in the office, our world class closer (defined as one in 500 sales people) said, "To make this a memorable day, lets celebrate your decision." Out of the mini fridge came an ice cold bottle of Dom Perignon champagne which was cracked open and a toast given to this magnificent day. "In your lovely new residence, may the best days of yesterday be the worst days of tomorrow!"

Now, that's world class selling. One final point; as the family was leaving, she took a Polaroid picture of them in front of their new high rise home! You have to agree this was surely a presentation for the ages – and why she was known as a legend in her own time.

When you quantify a Medal of Honor presentation, this one has all the ingredients.

TOM TALKS... About Killer Closes

I heard this one many years ago and put it into circulation. A sales lady was explaining the benefits of buying a new home versus an old used home. She landed on the killer – "Imagine it is the morning after the first night in your new used home. You wake up early. You sit on the edge of your bed. You look down at that avocado shag carpet and what do you see? You see someone else's toenails."

The story has been around awhile, but its graphic impact still works today.

Clipper

The Power of Persistence

Clipper Smith was a retired football coach from Penn State University and Villanova. He had scouted me in high school and we had discussed matriculating at Penn State. However, I chose a different institution. He was a master presenter and made every case for joining that august state college, not the least of which was the benefit of playing for a national power like the Penn State Nittany Lions. While it would have been a push for me to make the team, the invitation was enticing.

Years later I was vice president of sales and marketing for a company that later became the runner up volume builder of all publically held builders. Clipper Smith had retired from football and moved to the west coast as a sales executive for the giant, Title Insurance Company. He telephoned and invited me out to lunch where we reveled in some old football yarns. Then he asked if there was any way I could deliver some title insurance to his company. I told him I would try and proceeded to get the boss interested. There was no going. The 74 year old owner had engaged his present title company for several years, and since it was with an old college classmate, he declined to move any title business anywhere.

So, Clipper was dismayed but not disheartened. Throughout the year he would call me from time to time to see how I was doing. He sent me clippings of my old college team because Ivy League scores were hard to come by on the West Coast. He sent selective real estate articles to help me adjust to the California culture. Nary a week went by without some kind of contact from Clipper.

Now it was the end of the year. I was buying income property with five years pre-paid interest which was the norm of the day, but you had to get the property closed in the year of purchase in order for the incredible tax savings scheme to kick in. Those were the years when the federal government endorsed purchasing real estate property using five years of pre-paid interest on the mortgage of the building as a down payment for the property. Of course, as it was tax deductible interest, you could make a down payment with the money you would normally pay Uncle Sam. It was a heck of a deal and it really pumped the real estate market at that time.

I had this apartment building in Hollywood called Tudor Terrace under contract but it had to be closed by midnight December 31st. The problem was I wrote the contract December 30th and no title company said they could get it done in time – none except good ole Clipper. He rose to the occasion and said, "Let's see what we can do for you."

The contract was closed at 9:45 p.m. New Year's Eve. I was absolutely ecstatic over concluding this transaction. The day after New Year's, I told the boss what Clipper had done. He said, "If that man did that for you, I'll see to it he gets some of our business."

Sure enough, Clipper got his chance in one of our communities. His service was impeccable and the boss was pleased. So, Clipper got a second chance with another community, this one a tougher close. He kicked in his top closing clerks and they got the job done in record time. Of course, Clipper got the third job, and on and on until Clipper's company had all our business which was considerable.

Moral of this story is, follow-up, follow-up, follow-up. This was the consummate example of a professional salesperson never taking himself out of the selling game. He kept the information flowing, the camaraderie going, and ended up with every bit of our business thanks to his bulldog tenacity.

This story reminds one of Winston Churchill (often called The Bulldog) whose motto was, "Never, Never, Never quit."

When I'm asked what constitutes a great master closer? The answer is tenacity, the never quit attitude. After that, I called Clipper Smith the Comeback Kid!

Are you a closer or loser? Look at the word CLOSER. If you sell with Credibility, Confidence, Charisma, Consistency, and Closemanship, you are a CLOSER. Take off the letter C and what are you? A LOSER!

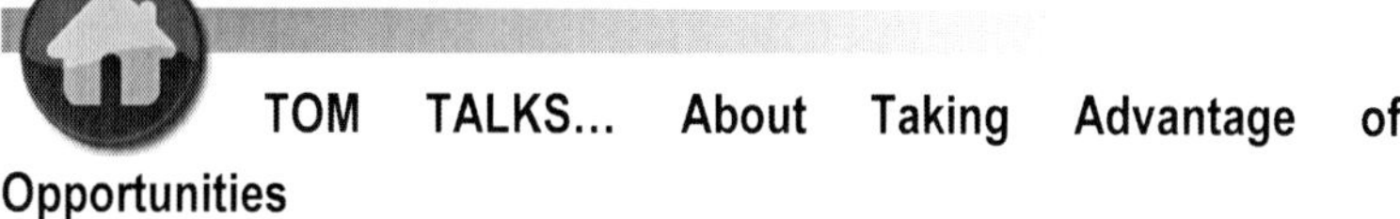

TOM TALKS... About Taking Advantage of Opportunities

It was a Broadway matinee on a Sunday afternoon. Hearsay had it the cast of *Les Miserables* was on top of their game. We were sitting about ten rows from the stage. Just before curtain time, the start of the play was delayed when a large commotion started in the back of the theater and proceeded down the aisle. There was a gentleman in a black hat, sunglasses, and an entourage of eleven kids proceeding to the seats right in front of us. He was escorted by six burly New York policemen. The little girl on my right exclaimed, "That's Michael Jackson sitting right in front of us. Boy, would I like his autograph."

The play started, and at the end of the first act, the legendary entertainer was escorted into a holding room because now everyone wanted his autograph. However, no one in the theater could get next to him. Policemen were guarding him. The children were around him. No one could reach the great performer except for me because I was sitting right behind him. Just before the second act the little girl said, "Please sir, would you help me get Michael Jackson's autograph? My name is Fay."

I leaned over, tapped Mr. Jackson on the shoulder and asked, "Sir, would you kindly give this little girl named Fay your autograph?"

He generously obliged writing on the program, "To my dear friend, Fay, Michael Jackson." Well, the little girl was beside herself. She had the autograph of the famous star. She was the envy of all the people in the theater and would be queen of the mountain when she got home.

Coming out of the theater, my wife exclaimed, "Wow, you really are a master closer. You were the only one in the theater who got his autograph."

I responded, "Let's set the record straight. There are two rules to closing sales. Rule Number One – to arrive at a one-of-a-kind or in this case, be in the right place. I was the only person in the theater with no one between us. Therefore, I was in the right place to ask for the sale. We call it one-of-a-kind in housing sales. Rule Number Two – you can be at the right place or at a one of a kind and not ask for the order. Recognizing I was in the right place, I did ask and as often happens, I did receive. Michael Jackson was a decent human being and was willing to give his autograph to the young girl."

The moral of the story: Sales are sales. Whether seeking an autograph or selling a new home, you have to be in the right place, and once there, you have to ask for the sale.

Slim

The Mysterious Wheel Estate Man

We were on a slow selling community one day doing a "Project Doctor." I was coaching an inexperienced salesperson when a young man named Slim rode into the parking lot on a tricycle – not your routine two wheeler but a three wheeler! He had funny looking shorts at half mast and a weird t-shirt. I must say, he looked quite comical with his jaunty tricycle helmet. These were $600,000 to a million dollar condominiums, and it was quite "obvious" to the uninitiated sales lady, this was not a buyer. She took the customer on a brief spin for about five minutes and brought him back with the salutation, "Thanks for coming in. Tell your friends about us."

I don't know what prompted me to do this, but I followed this castaway down to the parking lot and as he was mounting the tricycle seat, I said, "How about going on a brief tour?"

"Naw, I've seen enough," he said.

"C'mon. I'll get the golf cart."

"OK."

Somehow I persuaded him to join me in a brief tour of the outer reaches of the development where he had obviously not gone. Being a personable fellow, he enjoyed the ride over to the fringe area in our golf cart. I was trying to get a bead on who or what he was, but nothing was forthcoming. He was silent 'Sam the Clam.' When I explained our lower tier of condominium pricing and was finished demonstrating in the second building, our cavalier hippy became animated and said, "Let me come clean. This is my day off and I'm riding around on this silly tricycle. Good way to lose weight, you know. I'm really a broker for a major brokerage house in town and I'm farming this area. To tell the truth, I'm really excited about this unit right here. In fact, if you don't mind, I'd like to make a call to one of my friends who might be interested in this."

He made the call and tried to bring the friend out that day. When the prospect could not come, he suggested the following weekend. "OK" was the answer and I thought nothing of it until Wednesday of next week. Then I reasoned it might be interesting to call this guy and see if he was for real. I pulled out his business card and made the call Wednesday evening. Sure enough, he had forgotten about the incident, but upon reminding him of our conversation, he got animated one more time and said he would call her back and report the findings to me. That is exactly what happened. He called me back with the information he would bring her by at 10 a.m. Saturday morning whereupon the salesperson was notified and the sale was written.

Slim was a mind bender. While this was an extreme case, we must constantly remind ourselves that prejudging the customer can result in lost sales. How many sales are frittered away because sales agents judge the power of the vehicle without turning on the engine!

TOM TALKS... About Celebrating Sales Professionals

We should celebrate real estate sales professionals because they work harder than anyone else in the sales profession to make something happen. That "happening" influences the U.S. economy in a major way. Surveys have shown that when a new or resale home is sold, there is a chain effect of purchasing that reaches into many retail disciplines and that creates work! Let us all remember that housing can bring us into a recession and out of a recession. The key to economic prosperity is a proactive housing market and the salesperson is the one who drives this scenario.

At no point in the history of the housing industry has the salesperson and sales manager been more important to the health of the United States of America than right now.

Story 21

John

What Time Do You Set Your Alarm Clock?

John Long was the first 1,000 house home builder in the United States. The year was 1959. I was home building merchandising manager for *Life* Magazine. My job was to contact the top builders and see what building products they were using or would use to give *Life* advertising salesmen the opportunity to sell advertising to manufacturers like GE, Owens Corning Fiberglas, and American Standard. We would play back the success story to the manufacturer through the builder about the benefits of the product. The manufacturer would receive the playbacks and commit to more advertising. That was the bottom line. It was called "pull through" from the local level.

I couldn't wait to meet John Long who I heard possessed a work ethic beyond all others. When could I meet him? His right hand man said the only time or place I could see him would be on the job. Could I be out on the site at 5:45 the following morning? The next day at 5:45 a.m. sharp, I was being driven over to a single home on a cul-de-sac where the 1,000 house a year home builder was finishing an inspection. The sun had not yet come up, and Mr. Long was completing his inspection with a flashlight. It was incredulous to see this commitment to work in the field by such a successful entrepreneur. We had a wonderful interview. The highlight of that moment was what John Long said to me, "I can tell how successful a man is by what time he sets his alarm clock in the morning." I've never forgotten that simple homily. On holidays when the temptation to grab another forty winks is strong, I've always felt guilty and rose early. On workdays I wouldn't think of showing up to the office late because of the words of this role model. "Success is dependent upon how much quality time you are willing to invest in your dream," he went on to say.

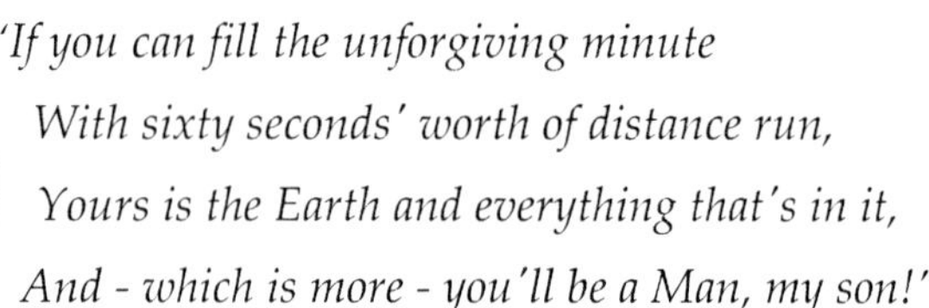

"If you can fill the unforgiving minute
With sixty seconds' worth of distance run,
Yours is the Earth and everything that's in it,
And - which is more - you'll be a Man, my son!"

~Rudyard Kipling

Anthony

I See My Homes Differently

There was a salesperson in the Midwest who was normally number three or four on a large sales staff. His ranking was consistent, not a flash in the pan. I thought nothing of this until I met this master closer and discovered he was legally blind. Imagine the shock of finding out there was a gentleman selling new homes that could only see fuzzy outlines. He had to walk with a stick. Someone had to drive him to work. There was no touring a prospect through the community. He had to rely upon his prowess as a master demonstrator of his models in order to position his product above the competition. During role plays, you would never know he was blind except for his cane and slight uncertainties. Best of all, you wouldn't know he had a disability due to his positive mental attitude. One time I asked him what made him perform so far above the others. His answer was a classic.

"Mr. Richey, I see my model homes through a different set of eyes. I've had to work very hard to learn the floor plans, to know where the furniture is so I wouldn't look foolish stumbling over it. I had to understand how the home sits on the site. I had to see the colors through the theater of my mind even if I couldn't see them myself. I don't believe I've used this disability as a crutch in any way. I believe I've sold houses through my sheer love of selling and the passion to help people."

This was a quote I wrote down at the time and I've carried it with me all my life. "I see my home through a different set of eyes." So often, we don't know how blessed we are with our health, eye sight, our rational minds, our work ethic, our trainability, and even in today's tough world, our positive mental attitude. When times get tough, think to yourself, "How would I sell homes if I were blind?" Remember, there is one salesperson out there that sees his homes through a different set of eyes.

You cannot depend upon your eyes when your imagination is out of focus.

~Mark Twain

Kenny

The Referral King

Kenny was an ex-Baylor quarterback who holds numerous Southwest Conference passing records. Most of all, he was an involved and consummate sales professional. Kenny was licensed to me for five years selling a community in Fort Worth, Texas. In my mind, this master closer's Medal of Honor presentation was represented by a number of planned selling events he conducted for nearly four and a half years. I call it "Booking tours with owner-endorsers."

Here's how it worked. Once Kenny had his owners happily moved into their new homes, he would arrange to bring them and their friends out to his community for a multi-dimensional tour. The deal was the owners had to bring their friends, remain for the tour, and end up sitting through the closing process. To sweeten the pot, Kenny would offer a catered breakfast at the country clubhouse which he paid for himself. Then, a boat ride on a pontoon boat traversing the lake, and perhaps a few holes of golf or even a game of tennis would be on the agenda. The key point was Kenny had an ironclad appointment every Saturday morning at 9 a.m. to tour his property with the owners and their friends. The residents and their buddies would arrive, take a tour, eat breakfast, enjoy the lifestyle, and Kenny would end up with a presentation of some field models, which the owners would insist their friends purchase. Why the endorsement? They wanted their golf or tennis partners close to them, or their kids had bonded together, or they wanted to share rides to work. There were many reasons happy owners brought their friends for a "Kenny" presentation.

As we were winding down the project, I asked Kenny to calculate what his incidence of closing was with this simple program. Believe it or not, it was just under 50%. In other words, every month, nearly two sales were made through this orchestrated program. Isn't it nice to commence a selling weekend with a contract and check sitting on the side of your desk? Kenny knew the power of the hot hand in football and used that consistently with this Medal of Honor coun<u>sell</u>ing process.

The 1-4-1 Referral Code

"I will write **1** referral sale **4** every **1** new home I sell."

Story

24

Van

Branding Yourself

Likewise, there was a new home salesman of Vietnamese origin who one day got smart. He said, "Why don't I advertise my personal self and my community in the Vietnamese newspaper and do it in my native language?"

So, he did. Every week there would be an ad with his photograph and a very simple message: "My name is Van. I sell new homes. I understand what you are looking for in a new home. Please give me an opportunity to visit with you. Come see my furnished models at a day and time of your convenience. I will be happy to serve you any way possible. Thank you."

In any given year, this simple program produced between twenty and thirty sales with a marketing budget of about sixty bucks for an ad which was paid for personally.

Now that is truly worthy of a Medal of Honor sales designation.

Every Salesperson Has ...

1. The RIGHT to a published ***Minimum Performance Standard*** (MPS).
2. The RIGHT to accurate and timely ***product and price information.***
3. The RIGHT to ***sales training*** and personal development programming.
4. The RIGHT to ***quality control***.
5. The RIGHT to professional ***service management and warranty work.***
6. The RIGHT to appropriate ***back-up staffing*** for high traffic times.
7. The RIGHT to professional ***sales management***.
8. The RIGHT to a periodic ***job assessment***.
9. The RIGHT to ***respect***.
10. The RIGHT to ***fair play***.

Craig

How a Negative Became a Positive

I had a salesperson selling lake front and lakeside building sites. He was a master closer by every definition you can imagine; great at the introduction, world class at the presentation, consistent in discovery, smooth and savvy with the objections handling, expert on preselling homes to fit on homesites, genuinely involved in ownership transfer through asking the right questions, and of course, he realized an extremely high level of closing. Indeed, Craig was a master closer or by definition, one out of a hundred salespersons at closing sales.

The problem with Craig was, he didn't like to wear neckties and he made that clear to the sales staff. As it turned out, we had a company dress code at the time that every salesperson had to be attired in professional garb and a necktie was a must. No jeans, no open shirts. The necktie was the standard of excellence. Craig refused to wear a necktie. How do you solve this dilemma?

A similar situation happened in the Kansas City Chiefs dressing room. A new addition to the team refused to pray with the team before the first game of the season. Coach Marty Schottenheimer was skilled at handling the situation. Through a series of overtures, he asked the player three times to pray with the team. When the player finally said, "What part of 'I don't pray,' Coach, don't you understand?" The coach thought fast and rather than de-motivate the team before an opening game said, "Son, why don't you go into that room next door and do whatever you do before a game, and the rest of us will get down on our knees and pray." I was there observing this and it was like a storm cloud had gathered, lightning was ready to strike, but through a creative answer, the crisis was avoided.

Back to Craig. The answer to the sales professional was comparable. No one should ever lose a master closer over a necktie. There was no way we would lose a master closer of that stature even though, as we've seen throughout this book, Medal of Honor discipline must prevail. There had to be a more sensible answer. That answer turned out to be as simple as this. We announced to the sales staff that anyone who could sell and close to the level of Craig's efficiency could also go without a necktie. If that was a big deal at the time, we made it a reward. Sell seven homes a month and you don't have to wear a necktie either. It became a goal to be reached. While it didn't satisfy my personal preference in the matter, it was a way of avoiding the catastrophe of losing a one in a hundred salesperson. The salespeople did rise to the occasion and several did sell at levels which negated the necktie rule. The absence of a necktie became a reward!

Whether it is selling, sales managing, building, administrating, motivating, or compensating, everyone in the sales and sales management game must understand that working with people introduces shades of gray that must be addressed. Creativity is king.

TOM TALKS... About the PROFESSIONAL Salesperson

P Plans

R Researches

O Organizes

F Follows up

E Executes

S Sells

S Services

I Involves

O Observes

N Neutralizes

A Attitudes

L Listens

Kenny (again)

Are You Turning Right or Left?

How about another "Kenny" sales Medal of Honor story! At the end of the working day, four of the five salespersons would drive out of the sales office driveway and turn right. The road to the right led out the front gate and home to their families. Kenny, who had a family too, turned left. Turning left meant that Kenny would drive slowly through the community, stopping when he saw a home owner and visiting with them about inconsequential things. And, of course, at the end of every chat there was a call to action. "By the way, I haven't seen you bring a friend in lately. Who do you know that needs a new home?" There was always a pleasant jab for a referral sale at the end of the pleasantries. Kenny got a lot of referrals. In any given time period, he would realize approximately 40% of his total sales brought to him by happy owners. "Turning left" or touring a community before you go home, especially during daylight savings time, might be the answer to an increase in sales production.

TOM TALKS... About Rushed and Rude Prospects

Often we are confronted with dilemmas such as a husband and wife who come storming in saying they only have two minutes. Your answer may be, "Let me review in two minutes what we have here in this price range that no one else has and then I'll let you browse at your leisure."

Another comment might be they only have ten minutes. Your answer could be, "Curious, last week a prospect said the same thing and now they are one of our happy owners." Or, a husband and wife are in the car and send the child in to get a brochure. Here you may elect to compliment the child, hand the child a brochure, and walk out to the car to create a reason to tour the model. You have to be careful you don't get too enthusiastic. "Please don't confuse my enthusiasm for any kind of pressure. You should check out our model because you really can't judge the floor plan by the brochure. You have to experience it yourself. Let's look at it, shall we?" Keep your cool!

Carl & Lydia

A Glass "Half Full or Half Empty"

I was talking to an old client who had heard me say eighteen years ago that any salesperson who distributes fifty business cards a week, or two hundred business cards a month, should realize not less than ten on site tours and with reasonable closing skills, one sale. Having pushed that idea so many years, I felt a reprieve when he said it still worked eighteen years later.

As the owner of a small but prosperous company, he related how difficult it was to get sales people to do this even though it would deliver twelve more sales per year which would bring them a vacation in Paris, France, not Paris, Texas. And, there's a big difference! The problem he relayed was that he couldn't get sales people to do it.

I had a particularly strong sales staff I was addressing one day and I asked this staff of approximately twenty-five people if someone would volunteer to hand out 200 business cards a month with a salutation at the end, "By the way, who do you know that is looking for a new home." A young man named Carl volunteered. He was new to the industry, eager, bright-eyed with the proverbial bushy tail, and swore to me on the honor system he would hand out 200 cards in the next 30 days. I was excited about the outcome. Unfortunately, Carl ran out of gas about the second week, and although he had booked some onsite presentations, he wasn't sure it was worth the effort. So, he quit the endeavor. Today, he's looking for a job.

At the same time, I had a sales lady in the South named Lydia who had agreed to pass out business cards on the basis that if she got a sale, we'd pay her a hundred dollar spiff. Imagine my glee when she informed me she had sold not one, but two sales. Management gave her a $200 good faith bonus.

What was the difference between the two? Simple. Positive mental attitude. Lydia knew it would happen and willed it to happen. She believed her "glass" was half full. The young man, Carl, through his negative mental attitude, thought the "glass" was half empty. Today that lady is a master prospector and valued closer. And Carl? He has drifted off into the abyss of non performing naysayers.

J. Douglas

Silence Can Close!

J. Douglas Edwards was the consummate sales trainer. No one was better, including the legendary Dave Stone. I used to bring J. Douglas into our sales and marketing sessions in Southern California when I was chairman of the SMC of Los Angeles, Orange, and Ventura Counties. Doug had the all time Medal of Honor method of communicating the power of closing. He would say, "Whenever you ask the closing question (voice gets lower) … Whenever you ask the closing question (voice whispers) … Whenever you ask the closing question (voice shouting) SHUT UP! The first one who talks, loses!" If anyone was falling asleep or not taking notes, this would get their attention real fast! I remembered well that admonishment when I was selling a real estate investment trust to the chairman of the board in his well appointed penthouse office suite. We went back and forth on the benefits of the proposition. I was anchoring my U-benefits tightly and launched the closing question. This led right up to the final close, "Let's get started, shall we?" As Doug instructed, after I asked the closing question, I shut up. But the chairman shut up too. Seconds went by and I was still silent. More seconds went by and he was silent. Minutes went by with total silence on both sides. It may have been only fifteen minutes, but it seemed like an hour when he finally let out a giant roar and said, "I read the same book you did!" But, he bought!

Some of the things you read about or hear from trainers may seem off the wall, but don't scoff at them until you try them. Keep an open mind. As Alec Baldwin in the landmark movie *Glengarry Glen Ross* said, "Remember the ABCs ... Always Be Closing."

TOM TALKS... About One-of-a-Kind

Closing is duck soup if you remember you first must achieve one-of-a-kind. That's defined as the one right home at the one right time in the one right location at the one right price and terms – and when it's gone, it's gone! Testing for a one-of-a-kind is reflected in these questions: "Can you see yourself living here?" Or, "Can we call this your one-of-a-kind?" Or, "In your shopping, have you found any home anywhere that you like better?" Positive responses reflect that one-of-a-kind has been achieved. Now you can final close.

Story

29

Bill

Creativity Knows No Boundaries

A.L. Williams, football coach turned insurance magnate had it right when he said; "All you can do is the best you can do." What he meant was that if you give the project or challenge everything you have 100% of the time with clear and focused accountability, you cannot hold yourself responsible for a negative outcome. You have in fact done everything you could.

There are some sales people in our society that don't feel that way. They expect business to come to them or they expect a lay down to happen at the close. This is not the real world in today's economy. Today you have to really scrounge for business. You have to be creative in the sense that you cause many disciplines to work for you, not against you. In fact, you may cross lines between new home sales and resales.

To underscore this point, let's go to Denver, Colorado where a professional sales counsellor named Bill Watson holds forth. Let's see how Bill thought and worked outside the box to make a sale happen.

Bill had the listing on the old home of a buyer who wanted a new home. In order to sell the existing home, the buyer was in a $14,000 negative equity position on the old home and only had $7,500 to apply to the old property. (Anybody can contribute to the negative on the closing of the old home). What the sales pro did was provide an agent credit of $7,000 to the sale of the old home. The buyer came to the table with $7,000; the sales pro came with $7,000. The builder paid the salesperson 6% to sell the new home and the sales pro contributed $7,000 towards the negative equity of the old home.

Simply said: the sales professional provided an agent credit of $7,000 on the sale of the old home and received a 6% co-op commission on sale of the new home, donating 3% to get the old home sold and keeping 3% for his efforts. Now that's creative selling!

"Reality can be beaten with enough imagination."

~Anonymous

Cynthia

The Queen of Closing

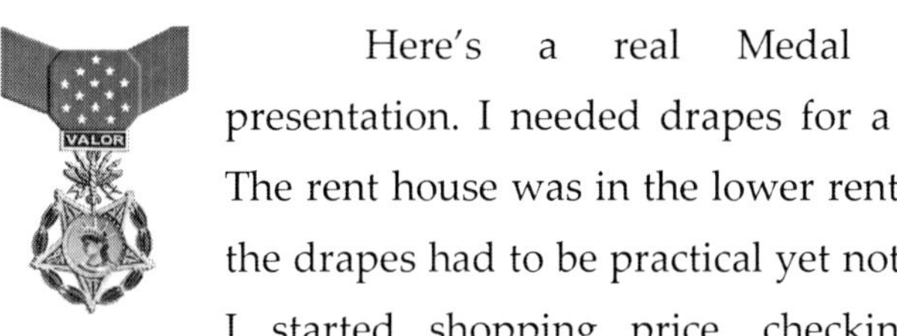

Here's a real Medal of Honor presentation. I needed drapes for a rent house. The rent house was in the lower rental ranges so the drapes had to be practical yet not glamorous. I started shopping price, checking the ads, eliminating the retailers until I found if I drove hard I could lower the price. The price seemed to get lower as I gained experience in negotiating a deal. After six or seven retailers, I entered a nondescript looking store where a young lady bounced to the door and greeted me with enthusiasm, "Bet you are looking for drapes, correct?"

"Yes," I answered.

"For your personal residence or something other."

I countered, "A rent house."

"Oh, we sell a lot of rent house drapes here. If you don't mind, let me ask you a few questions."

"Great," I answered.

"First of all, what is the monthly rent of your property?"

I gave her the answer.

Next, "What's the exposure to the sun?"

I answered, "Come to think of it, the window wall on the leisure side of the home faces west."

"Good," she answered. "How about the color of your carpet?"

"Chocolate brown. Why do you ask?"

"Oh, it's important to keep your tenants happy. The drapes must match the carpet." Then she asked a question I had never heard before. "Do you happen to have the measurements of your windows?"

"Come to think of it, I do."

"That's fabulous," she said with excitement. "Now we can go to the ready made department." Then she launched her big gun. "Sir, if you think you've come to my store to buy the cheapest drapes in town, that won't happen. But what I will provide for you is a drape that will hold up far longer than the standard drape you buy in discount stores. Why? Because we have a brand new material with a special sunlight protection and wear resistance that will triple the life of these window hangings. Wouldn't it be ideal not to have to replace your drapes if you change tenants or sell the property?"

I had to admit yes.

Then she moved into matching ready made drapes of a beige/chocolate brown color with my dimensions. By the time she was finished, she compiled a drape package that was approximately one-third more than the lowest price I had shopped. However, she said, "We have a one year guarantee on this material and if you see any fading during that time, come back and we'll exchange them."

This was the factoid that closed the sale. This complete belief in her integrity and the fact that I was buying a higher quality drape that would last longer caused me to buy the complete set, convinced I was doing the right thing. Right thing it was! That set of drapes lasted until I sold the rent house several years later. The tenants were happy and I did not have to replace one drape during that period.

Sometimes we have to remember, selling begins when the customer says your price is too high. Closing begins when the customer asks for your discount. The contract is written when the salesperson asks if they are interested in quantity or quality. Focusing on true value for true price wins in most sales situations. And remember: WIN means **W**rite **I**t **N**ow!

Earl

Perfect Practice Makes Perfect

There is a professional sales manager for a giant New York Stock Exchange company who adamantly believes in role playing. When he was learning the ropes, he was the first in line to role play and has subsequently felt each salesperson should pay their dues. While sales people do not like role playing, (we call it sales simulating), it is a way of learning the trade. Where would baseball players be without batting practice, football players without scrimmages, speakers without practicing their deliveries, and actors without rehearsing their lines? We live in the day of drill, practice, rehearse, and Earl Robinson is the chief proponent.

When doing a sales training program for Earl, you know one thing, his staff will be motivated and energized to participate in sales simulations and you as a trainer, will be expected to do role modeling. The role modeler takes the position of the salesperson and simulates a typical presentation from A to Z or module to module. One of the most effective role modeling exercises is for the sales coach to put himself or herself in the position of the salesperson, and then ask the sales staff to throw every real world objection they have heard at the role modeler. The sales staff loves to see how their boss would handle a tough situation to stump the expert if you will. If the sales trainer/coach is good, they should be able to handle all contingencies with professionalism.

One of the best ever at this is a professional sales manager in the mid-West called John. John is from the old school, admittedly, but exercises the principles of blocking and tackling through an extensive drilling, practicing, and rehearsing regimen. If you are not willing to put on the pads, so to speak, in John's environment, you don't sell with his team.

The interesting thing about learning is that more salespeople come to a seminar <u>not</u> to learn than to learn. Having given hundreds if not thousands of seminars in my life over a fifty year span, it is amazing how many sales people sit in the back rows of a training room, conversely, isn't is curious the top stars often sit in the front rows. The super stars come to learn. The newbies come to hide. One could argue this is not always true, but from my experience, it is more true than not. Here is a statistic sales people should know: When a trainee sits in the front row, they learn 14% more than if they sit in the back row.

I recently had a training session with a master closer in Canada I had trained many years ago. Duncan sits in the front row with several pens fully loaded, lots of pads, ready to make notes. Boy, does he challenge. If he doesn't agree with the trainer's premise, he says so. If he does agree, he says so as well. He contributes and learns. In the words of Francis Bacon, "Conference makes a ready man or woman." By that, Bacon alluded to participation creates learning, and learning hones skills. And skills, write contracts.

TOM TALKS... About Assumption

You simply assume the prospects have come in to purchase a new home. You **bond** with that assumption. You **discover** with that assumption. You differentially demonstrate -- particularly your style and design -- with that assumption. You **neutralize** objections with that assumption. You **close** with that assumption. And, if they don't buy on the initial visit, you **follow up** with that assumption until they buy or die!

Assumption is at least 50% of the closing process. Master closers understand this principle and that's why persistence is their middle name.

Story

32

Lou

Heroes All!

I wonder if salespersons know what an important part they play in a family's life. Very often they become the hero to a family who purchases a home from them. The buyers won't communicate this to the salesperson, and often they show irritation if the builder doesn't deliver expectations on time. However, in the last analysis, there is always a warm spot in a homebuyer's heart for the salesperson who sells them their first property or their destination home.

I remember when I bought my first real estate property. It was a four story, brick apartment building in downtown Los Angeles where a master closer named Lou Lepp insisted this was necessary for my portfolio. I wiggled and waffled and didn't come to closure until a competing buyer appeared. Lou was honest with his close. "You can take ownership or you can let the other buyer have it. However, let's look at the benefits…"

Magically, as Lou laid out the benefits to owning this property and how much I could shelter my income, I got the message quite clearly. Real estate was one heck of a place to park your money. Eventually, I sold that building to buyer A with a wrap around mortgage who then sold it to buyer B with a wrap. In other words, I had two wrap around mortgages on the building, but Lou taught me an important principle of life: If you get your asking price, don't look back. Be satisfied with what real estate can do for you. Sales people across the United States who sell new or resale homes should understand, they become the hero to the homebuyers who have access to their skills. A family will never forget the sales professional who treats them well.

TOM TALKS… About What Makes a Salesperson Successful

Being Creative: Differentiation is fueled by creative sales presentations, hence no two home sales are ever the same. Question-based selling fosters creativity.

Persistence: Master closers possess a strong, healthy self-esteem which creates the resiliency to handle rejections.

Story 33

Audrey

Service IS Sales!

A large eastern builder had a community in Annapolis, Maryland that was stalled. Five sales people had tried to sell it and had failed. They were on the verge of hiring a new salesperson from outside the area. In the interview, I looked at the candidate and was reminded of Jessie James. We call them gun slingers, a highly paid and perhaps not so professional salesperson that comes in to clean up the inventory and then leaves with many challenges in their wake.

Before the hire was made, I asked the company to look within to see if anyone on the staff could get the job done. While reviewing the database one day, I heard the service person, Audrey, discussing the needs of her residents with an abundance of empathy. I turned to her boss and asked how long she had been on staff.

"Oh, she has been here for over fifteen years."

"Has she ever been given the chance to sell?"

"Not at all! Nobody thinks of her as a salesperson. She has done a wonderful job with service, her buyers love her to death, and that is her slot in the company."

"Does she make much money?" I asked.

"The standard compensation for a journeyman service person," was the answer.

Later I approached her and asked if she had any selling experience. Her answer was that years ago she sold automobiles and high end clothes at retail. In fact, she had quite a bit of training but not the training she felt she needed for new home sales.

"Mr. Richey, if you are thinking about me joining the sales staff, that would never work. I am good at service, but not at sales."

The challenge with her was confidence. Someone had told her that once a service person, always a service person. In fact, sales people are service people. If you don't service your buyers, you don't get referral sales. Referrals are <u>the</u> low hanging fruit of the housing industry, and they should be secured if the buyers are happy with the building, selling, and service process. The bottom line was we put her through an intensive training and development program, brought her up to speed, assigned her to the job, and she closed the community out in record time! How? Her happy owners helped her sell out by bringing their friends and family to the community. Her referral sales exceeded fifty percent!

TOM TALKS... About Service and Assumptive Closing

We had a robbery in our home, one of those nasty home invasions you want to forget about. It was an armed robbery and in the process of ransacking the house, the thieves needed a rope to tie us up. They pulled out the wires of my stereo and did just that, leaving the house with a pretty good haul. However, our lives were spared and that is all that mattered. When I had to get my stereo fixed, I called seven different stereo repair centers. All seven said they would charge me from $50 to $75 dollars just to come out and give me an estimate of what was required. The last contact was a gentleman named Felix Garza. When I asked what the fee was for the estimate, he said there was no charge. “Let me come out and see what I can do to help you.” When he arrived, Felix informed me the two wires could be acquired through the Bose Company. He gave me the website for the company and told me how to hook up the wires once I received them.

“How much?” I asked.

“Oh, nothing. That’s on me. No sense in charging you for something as small as this.”

As Felix was leaving, he noticed the speakers. “Let’s try these speakers and see what they sound like. They are the small Bose units and they may or may not work well in this room."

When we turned on the speakers, they didn't sound that good. Either they had been broken in the robbery or they had just worn out. Felix said, "Let me get you some new speakers for this room and I'll install them at no charge. If you don't like them, I'll take them back. If you do like them, I'll charge a nominal price. Fair enough?" We agreed. Felix came back and installed the speakers. We loved them and cut him a check for the price and installation.

Now Felix said, "You know, let's not throw these small Bose speakers out. Do you have a home office?"

I said, "Sure, upstairs."

"Well, let's go up and see if they work up there."

He installed the speakers and suggested I needed a new unit to play multiple CDs. If I didn't like the system, there would be no charge. Like it I did! The speakers were perfect for that size room so I cut him another check.

Three days later Felix called me on the phone. "Mr. Richey, I bet your outside speakers may not be working correctly unless you have a special installation."

"Well, what are you getting at?"

"Let me come out and test your outside speakers and put in some new ones. If you don't like the sound, you don't pay me." Now, secretly I knew my outside speakers were blown out; why not give Felix another chance. So, out he came and installed the new speakers to my utter delight. Felix was given another check.

Later, he called me again. "You know, Mr. Richey, I was thinking. In order to get those pool side speakers modulated correctly, you have to go into your house in a wet bathing suit dripping on your nice wood floor, isn't that correct?"

"Yes," I said.

"Let me come out and put a volume control on the outside speakers so you won't have that problem."

"Ok, Felix, my good man, come on ahead."

I was happy with the work and wrote Felix another check.

My goodness – what a professional! In a down economy where I absolutely vowed and cast in bronze that I would not spend incremental dollars, Felix drilled through that resolution. He did it with the sheer power of assumptive closing. His assumption was that if he brought the right equipment and installed it at a fair price and it conveyed an improved lifestyle, he would be rewarded. It's the same principle in home sales. Sell and service the buyer and you'll receive more business. Our economy needs more "Felixes" in the world of new or resale home sales.

There is a post script. An electric storm blew out my big screen TV. Guess who will get the retail order and the fee for wiring and installing a new home theater?

Men are rich only as they give. He who gives great service gets great rewards.

~Elbert Hubbard

Story 34

Linda

Who's the Chef in the Family?

I heard this Medal of Honor presentation and have never forgotten it. In fact, it is the central point of kitchen presentations we train with today. Rummaging around a model home I heard the salesperson say, "Mr. and Mrs. Jones, who's the chef in the family?" The husband raised his hand said, "I am."

The salesperson persisted, "Mary, since Jimmy is the chef in the family, what's your role in the kitchen?"

She answered, "To make hors de oeuvres and take care of the wine."

"Oh, so you're the wine steward? Is that correct?"

She agreed.

Back to the husband, "Jimmy, what's your specialty?"

The husband gleefully answered, "Italian lasagna."

"Got any special recipe?"

The answer was, "Sure, crab meat lasagna. It'll knock your socks off. I found my special recipe in Venice, Italy."

Then the salesperson launched a customer oriented presentation of her kitchen.

"How does this open space appeal to you?"

"Great," the couple said.

"The benefit here is you can prepare your meal and hors de oeuvres while you are talking with your guests. Look good?"

"Great," they said.

"What type of plan do you have in your kitchen today? Is it L-shaped, U-shaped, or perhaps a double galley?"

"Oh, it's a U-shape," the husband offered. "The trouble is everything seems to back up at the end of the U." The wife concurred and said they were looking for an L-shape plan with an island.

"Got it!" The salesperson answered. Next she queried, "What's your biggest complaint about your present kitchen?"

Husband and wife jointly answered, "Poor lighting."

"Let's count the light sources," the salesperson asked. "How many do you see in this award winning Rich-built kitchen?"

As the couple counted, the salesperson concluded there were six artificial light sources and three natural sources for a combination of nine overall. "Light is our middle name." she gently suggested.

The next step was to confirm the abundance of storage. "Do you ever have enough storage in the kitchen?"

The couple answered with a "no" to which the salesperson opened the pantry door with a flourish which revealed a walk-in pantry with adjustable shelving. Also she pointed out the cabinetry was 42 inches tall with adjustable shelving and space above the refrigerator for a wine rack. Now the couple was in complete agreement.

The appliances were described through the question based process. "What types of appliances do you have now? Ever been frustrated with the service? What particular color would appeal to you? Share with me what you would like your next kitchen to look like regarding appliances?"

The couple responded to these questions and decided the appliance upgrade in stainless steel would be just perfect.

Then the salesperson moved into the eating possibilities. "This is not our Plan 2033 with the A elevation," she confirmed. "This is our four eating area home. Look! There is formal dining over there with enough space for a ten seat table and over here we have snack bar eating and right by the patio, an area for morning breakfast eating. Of course, half a step outside there is the grilling or barbecue eating area. Call this our four eating area home. Have we found a plan that works for you? What do you think?"

Here was a presentation loaded with questions moving people toward a decision through sales leadership. The final point was the flooring. Here she pointed out the flooring was unique and special, and of course, available in different types of colors, materials, and sizes through the design center. She wrapped it up with this close. "Based on what you've agreed to so far, it looks like we've found your dream kitchen. Is that correct?"

They answered, "Yes."

"Why don't we call this your personal gourmet kitchen, or better yet, your dramatic entertainment center?"

They agreed again.

"Now," she suggested, "Let's take time out for just a minute, close our eyes, and smell that crab meat lasagna which you have baking in your oven, shall we?"

The family closed their eyes, they smelled, and they bought!

In the early years a major appliance manufacturer had this slogan, "If the wife buys the kitchen, the family buys the home." Now with household duties being shared between husband and wife, it has been revised to, "If the family buys the kitchen, the family buys the home."

TOM TALKS... About Filling the Database

In an uncertain economy, *when the going gets tough, the tough get going*. Years ago, sales staffs worked six day work weeks. Today, some of the top producers are taking one day off per week and devoting that time to off site prospecting. They locate possible buyers, brokers, and influencers that can direct them to a potential home buyer. They make their calls from morning to night and write call reports about where they've been. Often, sales management shares the load by making calls in concert with the salesperson. The database is filled, worked, and an onsite tour and possible sale realized. The goal of every home selling professional is, 'never let a week go by without registering at least ten new families." If the market or marketing only brings five, the sales professional makes up the difference with their own efforts. Watch that pipeline. It should never fall below five "A" prospects or ten "B" prospects.

An "A" prospect is defined as ready, willing and able to buy somewhere within 30 days. A "B" prospect has one of the ready, willing & ables missing and will buy somewhere within 120 days.

Jim

Land Those Sales!

One of my all time heroes in the front line of home sales is Jim Lee who was the 1990 National Salesperson of the Year for the National Sales & Marketing Council of the National Association of Home Builders. Jim is the model of discipline, personal training, empathy execution, proper use of ego, and the knowledge of when to close them and when to fold them. It is not unusual to see Jim Lee at a home builder's convention walking down the aisle with a couple of hundred dollars of educational books purchased from the Builder Bookstore. Jim Lee always sits in the front row at training sessions and always takes notes. Jim is a master of assessing each and every presentation in a made sale-lost sale analysis. Jim feels that no matter how good you are, you can never be good enough. For a small builder in the Minneapolis area,

Hans Hagen Homes, he consistently earns top dollar because of his attention to process and detail.

One time we were talking about what it takes to be a highly productive home salesperson and Jim recited this incredible message.

"You know, Tom, sometimes I feel like the traffic controller at La Guardia Airport in New York. I have a number of planes in the sky all flying toward the same runway at one time. I have to land those planes with perfect safety and with the ultimate in control. Liken that to a number of prospects that I have circling around my homes, some willing to buy, some not so sure. My job is to land those prospects onto a specific home and satisfy them totally with their purchase. I have to control their purchasing disciplines until they make a successful choice. Then I have to manage with follow through the things they require me to do, similar to a ground controller who takes over from tower control and guides the airplane into a hangar.

"For example, after I take you to the airport, I have to go back to the community and meet a possible buyer at 7 p.m. Tomorrow at 9:30 a.m., I'll be touring a prospect family toward a possible sale. In the afternoon, I'm looking forward to a come back appointment on their fourth visit. I've strategized a way to bring them to closure with this visit. I believe my planning will do the trick! You see, the bottom line is there are various factions and entities that cause sales to happen. Some are physical and some are couched in people. If you are on top of your game, you know how to control all possibilities and bring success home. Flight controllers have to deal with the intangibles of weather, errant piloting, delayed flights, maintenance issues, and a number of abstract things to bring success to the enterprise. Sales people do too. I've learned selling homes is not unlike being a flight controller at a major airport."

What incredibly sage words from a true legend in his profession.

TOM TALKS... About Siting

Something magical happens when sales counselors go on site with their prospects. Call it ownership transfer. The mystique of communing with the land may be part of it, or the synergy of sight, sound, smell, and touch, call it the lifestyle experience. Or simply, call it the clearing of the mind through the wind in the face. Also, the homesite is where the one-of-a-kind lives. The Realtor code of Ethics starts ... "Under all is the land." The character of the land, developed building site, view, vista, flora, fauna, clean air, quiet, or simply the invitation to a new lifestyle is the alchemy that creates one-of-a-kind gold. Heed this message: "Closing happens where ownership transfers and that is clearly in or on the property the prospects, who have now transitioned to home buyers, step up and purchase!"

Story

36

Sally

The Incognito Buyer

Sally, the sales manager, was manning a downtown lifestyle community for a salesperson one day when a gentleman walked in with casual clothing and a stand-offish attitude. He informed her he wanted to see her highest priced line of homes. He was extremely aloof and non committal. On an average to medium traffic day he may not have been given much time. He certainly didn't seem interested and he wouldn't reveal his loan qualifications. However, Sally persisted in her presentation until he got excited over a particular residence. There it was, ready to go, just asking to be sold! He stepped forward and asked what he needed to do to take this home off the market. Sally told him she needed a $5,000 check. The gentleman responded with "I don't have

$5,000 to give you right now, but I'd like to reserve it until Monday."

Sally always had a rule that it was far better to bring an urgent buyer to contract now than take a hold deposit. So, she informed him the home would be on the market until he could make the required deposit. Then he asked if she would do him a favor and keep it off the market for one day. Sally said she couldn't do that but would do her best to sell customers into alternate properties until he could get back to her on Monday. Then she looked him in the eye and asked, "Are you for real? Do you really want to follow through with this purchase?"

He looked her in the eye and responded, "Trust me, I'm a buyer."

She really didn't think it was a sale until she got a call at 9 o'clock Monday morning. The call was from an attorney. The caller proceeded to say, "You had a purchaser in there Saturday who wanted to buy such and such residence. I trust it is still available."

She acknowledged it was.

The attorney said, "We'll be over before noon with a cashier's check for the full price."

Just before noon, an entourage of attorneys arrived, flyspecked the agreements, and produced a cashier's check. When she queried about this unusual event, she was told the purchaser was the owner of a major mortgage company, was enduring a brutal divorce, could not take any of his funds out of hiding to make the purchase, so he was buying the home through his company until he could take personal title.

Every salesperson has had this happen to them in some way or other. The important point is professional sales people have to possess the attitude that the more mysterious a buyer is, the more viable they may be. Every salesperson with any reasonable tenure will have experienced the seemingly non-qualified buyer who rides in on a motorcycle, or drives up with a clunker, or expresses interest in a pricey product while wearing dog-eared jeans and a ragged t-shirt -- and then calls later to buy it.

Here is an example. You are selling a pricey lifestyle product in the Palm Springs area. A shaggy prospect with an old blue sweater arrives at 4:30 pm and wants a tour. The job closes at 5:00 p.m. Two salespeople refuse to tour him saying the project is almost closed. You step up and take him on an abbreviated spin through the property. He sees a site he likes and writes you a check for $2,900,000. You look at the name in the upper left hand corner. It's the name of a computer icon well known throughout the world. Don't over or under qualify!

"How many sales have been written with presentations that started five minutes before closing time?"

~Tom Richey

Michael

Efficient Engines Require Oil

There was a sales manager for a resort project north of Dallas that understood motivation. John was blessed with a salesperson named Michael. On a five person sales staff, Michael sold more property than the other four put together. He was a selling dynamo. Michael hit a speed bump. In short order he incurred five cancellations at one time. With this he was devastated. The enlightened sales manager, John, realized this world class closer (one out of five hundred) was fried with burn out. He insisted Michael take five days off. When he resisted saying he had to get the sales back, John insisted it was time to take off or incur permanent time off. He counseled Michael that he didn't want to see Michael's smiling face anywhere near the job site. "Get lost for five days," John said and Michael was forced to agree. He came back with his batteries charged and made up the five cancellations in no time.

There are two lessons here. Jim Brown, the great football player, confided he always jogged back to the huddle slowly because if he was seriously hurt, the defense wouldn't know and wouldn't key on him. So, he jogged back at the same pace all the time to camouflage an injury. In short, he confused the defense. The parallel with Michael is when you run into negativity, purge it out of your system, recharge the batteries, and remember there may be times you have to rethink and re-plan your sales strategies. Then, return to the fray refreshed.

As a footnote, Michael was the only salesperson I've ever seen who could walk onto a wooded property and describe every species of flora on that site. It served him well when he needed to differentiate from competing recreation land and lots sales people.

The secret of his success was when he left the restaurant business to enter real estate, he understood the power of achieving success through other people. He called it OPE, the power of Other People's Effort. So, he farmed the area surrounding his large development from convenience store operators to bankers to gas station attendants, to other real estate agents, to influentials of any size or type whereupon when customers drove through the area and stopped somewhere, they were given Michael's business card. To this day, he rarely takes floor traffic since the majority of his business is driven via appointments made through his off site spheres of influence.

TOM TALKS... About Taking Time for Humor

Here's a true story which I don't believe was a comic routine. I was in San Francisco waiting for a flight to Washington, D.C. The intercom announced that flight No. 1 was canceled for mechanical reasons. A few minutes later, we boarded airplane No. 2. Once we were comfortably seated, another voice came over the intercom saying our second flight was canceled because of mechanical difficulty. So, we all traipsed off the airplane. While we were waiting for the third flight, I spotted the pilot, approached him with a smile, and said, "Sir, as a pilot, aren't you concerned about all these mechanical break downs?"

His answer was, "Damn concerned! That's why I'm getting out of flying. I'm retiring in three months."

"Oh, you're retiring in three months. Why?"

The reply came back, "It's damaging my health. I'm drinking more than usual."

"What do you plan to do after you retire from the airline business?" I asked.

Without missing a beat he replied, "To continue my full time job."

"What's that?"

"I'm a home builder!"

I couldn't resist, "Wow, you have two high risk occupations – flying airplanes and building houses."

Scott

The Fine Art of Fading Objections

When they asked Wayne Gretzky, the all time great hockey player what made him successful, he answered, "I skate to where the puck is going, not where the puck is." Now relate that to sales. Great sales people plan their presentation for the contingencies of the buyer and build a case for purchasing which they can use later to close. This is done through question-based selling – playing the counselor's role – and astute listening. It is like skating to where the puck is going, not where it is.

Scott McClellan, the great hockey player from Canada who was the side kick of the Boston Bruins' Bobby Orr, says he learned how to escape injury by falling away from the impact, not skating into the collision. He likens this to a sales presentation that should not attack an objection head on but should neutralize it with process. As an example, one should cushion it, agree with it, question it three or more times, and then find the answer or solve the problem. Then, Scott elaborates that once you've confirmed you've neutralized the objection, you close on it. Very often the disciplines that make one successful in sports, business, or education are the same disciplines with different labels that cause one to be successful in sales.

TOM TALKS... About Rejection

We deal with three types of rejections in housing sales. 1) **Stalls** ... "We want to think it over", 2) **Objections** ... 70% of all objections are couched in Dollars, Distance, Size, Schools, and Security. The home is priced too high or too low; the location is too far away or too close to something; the room is too big or too small; the schools are a challenge, and the location has a shaky track record on security, 3) **Conditions** ... they can prevent buyers from being able to buy, like poor credit, poor health, or an unstable job. Every home selling professional must be a whiz at asking friendly questions that depict the prospect family's 'buyability.' Discovery is the Siamese twin to closing. Master closers understand that when building and reinforcing the sales power of one-of-a-kind.

"A desire can overcome all objections and obstacles."

~Anonymous

Louise

Great Selling Has No Age Limit

Ryland Homes had a salesperson that was consistently in the top ten of the company nationwide. She was known to be an A.C.E closer. We define A.C.E. as Accountable, Concerned, and Expertised. We knew she was accountable, concerned, and a master counselor, but we were not sure about her energy because she was older than most sales people. Our concerns were dispelled after a mystery shop where she took our shoppers into the teeth of a severe windstorm, walking them onto a purchase target. There my shoppers were out in the elements, jogging over the property with this determined "young" pro. On the tape you could hear the raindrops on the plat map. You could hear the sucking sound as the rubber boots were extracted from the mud. You could almost hear my shoppers shivering.

However, at the appropriate time, she went for the agreement and achieved it. She closed the sale for which she received a happy stipend. While we endorse that buyers need to be comfortable when making a buying decision, it has often amazed me how few salespeople take customers to a homesite in severe weather to create and reinforce a one-of-a-kind.

Relative to this, we were in Edmonton, Canada in late December. Two feet of snow had just fallen. We suggested we all go onsite to practice homesite demonstrations. The entire staff confirmed they seldom took people to look at their homesites because of the severe weather. This was a good staff, yet, I wondered why. So I asked them if they would volunteer for a special exercise during the winter months. To train the effort, we went out to a homesite. I remember standing in front of this gorgeous piece of land. The wind was blowing, snowflakes falling, and the temperature was below freezing. I said, "Let's try something unusual. Let's find the four corners of the site by approximating the width and depth utilizing this plat map. Now, let's run the four corners of the site, come back, and sell the site using the trench or outline in the snow."

We practiced this several times and the sales staff had an "ah ha" moment. Throughout the winter selling season, do something the competition would not – take every possible customer to the building site and "trench" the homesite by jogging a trail in the snow. This they did and not by coincidence, that sales team enjoyed one of the best winter selling seasons ever. Was it the trenching that made it happen? I suspect it was!

TOM TALKS... About Trade Partners as Team Members

Sometimes great selling surfaces in strange places and unusual circumstances – like trade partners!

It was a bit after 7:00 a.m. on a job in North Carolina. I was touring construction with the operations vice president. As we approached a home in the framing stage, we saw a young framer talking to a husband and wife. As we approached, we heard the framer say, “Although I have worked with other builders over the years, I like this company best because they make me to do things at a higher level of quality. Let me show you how we frame a home well above code. Look at the high grade of lumber, the caulking and sealing around windows and doors, and the number of nails to a field of sheetrock. And, their superintendent stays on my tail and that’s cool. For my money, they’ve got the best construction in the area.”

We introduced ourselves and discovered this family had purchased a home the night before and got smitten with buyer’s remorse. They were returning to reinforce their decision. Who was the game saver in this scenario? The young framer who was selling quality construction. The lesson here is to make your trade partners part of your sales process. Request and respect their training. Compliment them on a job well done. Make them the lengthened shadow of your selling and your company, and close on a positive note.

I Asked the Master Closer

Tell me my friend, if you really can,
What possible type of woman or man
Would grab a tiger by the tail
And get a kick from a new home sale.
You laugh and say I entered sales
Cause I liked that better than driving nails.
Seriously though, there are reasons why
I like to help my prospects buy.
It's fun to sell the American Dream
To feel you're part of a national team;
To make our country the best housed nation
And give the family a firm foundation.
In selling, you're either up or down.
You learn to survive without a frown,
To take the verbal punch on the chin
And get up and go out and start selling again.
To work long hours day and night,
Closing contracts with all your might,
To be challenged and learn to love it,
To face rejection and rise above it,
To hear ten no's before you hear a yes,
Then see it cancel and have one sale less.
I asked the master closer in confidence,
Do you run for just the dollars and cents?
He said, "It's not the money that's good,
The pride of closing out a neighborhood,
Or even a note of appreciation,
Or a quota-busting celebration.
You see, only I really know
What makes the Master Closer go.
The ultimate goal is the bottom line
When the prospect says, "Where do I sign?"

~Rudyard Richey

Story

40

Wayo

The Ultimate Self Generator

Perhaps the greatest closer I've ever seen is a salesman in the Texas valley named Wayo Ruiz. Wayo was named Sales Manager of the Year while managing a fourteen person sales staff for a Lee Evans "Best Business Practices" award winning builder. The same year and at the same time, he was selling and closing 171 homes. Every one of these homes was self generated because he didn't want to take business away from his sales staff. Wayo would work long hours and utilize every effort possible to self generate sales.

Example. We were conducting a program in the Laredo Country Club. As we were set to start the second morning, Wayo appeared with a contract in hand. He admonished his sales staff, "Any one of you could have had this sale. After you all left last evening, I made the rounds of the country club and found the food service manager who was looking for a new home. We drove home, got the spouse, made some evening presentations, and closed the new home at 11 o'clock last evening by the rays of my flashlight."

Another time, I was going to dinner with Wayo and he asked to be excused for a few minutes. Before he sat down he circled through the restaurant and asked every person there, "By the way, who do you know who's looking for a new home?" He handed out business cards to give to their friends. After dinner, the guitar player was given a business card and subsequently purchased a home.

Several years ago when the Hummer was introduced as a personal vehicle, Wayo purchased one and drove it through his town of Laredo with the understanding that if anyone wanted a ride in the Hummer they had to take a sales presentation. The kids were told to bring their parents to the community after they got their ride in the vehicle. It became an event to ride in that huge monster and Wayo turned it into a prospecting source.

Lesson to be learned. Wayo was an ex law enforcement officer who decided to enter new home sales. He attended every training session of substance paying his own way. The training investment of all sales companies across the United States is an average of $18,000 per salesperson before they are allowed to sell – and they are in training for three and a half months. In the housing industry, that investment is less than $1,000 and training time is nil.

For a capital intensive business such as housing, that has to change. Profits of the future will come not from expanding markets, but from sleeping competitors!

Today Wayo is running a successful housing business with his brother and having a challenging but wonderful time doing it.

TOM TALKS... About Asking for the Order

Having attended many manufacturer building product presentations, I am always amazed at how little closing is done. For example, I was monitoring a presentation by a roofing tile manufacturer on a major builder in Texas. The presentation sailed along smoothly for forty-five minutes with lots of factual information given and questions answered. The builder here was happy with the information but it was obvious nothing was proceeding forward. As the three sales representatives, including the district manager and myself were getting ready to leave, I stepped out of my role and said, "Hey folks, how are we going to wrap this one up?" The district manager asked, "What do you mean?"

I said, "Well, we haven't gotten any commitment from this builder about using our tile. Let me ask this purchasing director one question. Do you see the benefit of using concrete tile on your Texas houses?"

The purchasing agent said, "I see tremendous benefits, but I think your tile is too expensive, factoring in the additional bracing that is required."

At this point, the district manager saw the light and asked this closing question. "You have a Fall Festival of Homes coming up in a couple of months. Will you let us test a tile roof on one of your parade homes?"

The purchasing director replied that it would make sense. "Frankly, we have been talking about tile roofs on our custom homes, but haven't made the leap yet. Tell you what, I'll reserve one of our featured homes for a tile roof and work it into our framing blueprints immediately. Fair enough?"

Of course, the district manager for the roof tile company agreed enthusiastically.

The model home was built. The traffic loved the tile roof. The home was sold before the opening. The company went on to add tile roofs to its build-to-suit and custom home collection and tile roof selections became a big part of its personalization program.

That is the power of a close!

"If your imagination leads you to understand how quickly people grant your requests when those requests appeal to their self-interest, you can have practically anything you go after."

~Napoleon Bonaparte

Story

41

Marlena

The Power of One More Close

We were discussing in a sales meeting how to gauge when it is appropriate to go for one more close versus one less. By close, we meant asking for the order. The consensus was that it was tricky at best and you must go by your instincts. The answer is based on experience; it is more of a feeling state. Sometimes one more close will alienate the buyer and it may be more appropriate to book an appointment for the next day while everything is still fresh in their minds. Or, it may be advisable to go for one more attempt to get consideration and signature on paper while the buying rhythms and desires are high. One of the sales ladies suggested that it may be appropriate to go for one more close rather than one less because you often don't know the hidden circumstances and can't find out. Here was her example.

A husband and wife entered the sales center of her age restricted community and said they had been looking at the community and were thinking about making a decision. Searching the records, she found it was the customers' second time back. When she moved toward the decision after a one-of-a-kind had been selected, she noted extreme resistance on the part of the wife. The husband was all for it, while the wife was definitely against it. As she moved closer to the close, the wife said, "We're absolutely not going to purchase here. It is not our type of buyer," alluding to the age restriction.

As Marlena continued on with the story, her instinct was to not close them now, but try for another day. Yet, the husband was persistent. He made it clear they were going to own there, so according to the husband's wishes, the wife co-signed the agreement. It was evident the wife was hostile. Marlena expected a cancellation, but to her surprise there was none. The sale funded, the couple moved in and she didn't hear from them for several months.

Seven months later the wife came in with an extremely contrite demeanor, saying, "I'm so sorry for the way I acted the day we bought our home here. I wanted to come in and apologize profusely. You see, what you and I didn't know was my husband was suffering from a terminal disease. He was given six months to live and he wanted to have a home where we could spend quality time together in an uplifting environment. That is precisely what happened. He passed away three weeks ago. Thanks to you, we had the most wonderful time together in our thirty-five years of marriage. Again, thank you so much for putting up with me."

There was barely a dry eye in the room when the salesperson was finished and everyone understood that perhaps, just perhaps, there may be that rare time when you sell and close against your inner feelings. In that particular instance, it was the time to write the agreement.

TOM TALKS... About Guarantees

In 1984 there was a sales lady in East Stroudsburg, Pennsylvania who talked her firm into giving her a $60,000 per year guarantee. This was at a time when few sales people earned $100,000 a year selling homes. I told the company, "Don't make that deal. It will do nothing but breed complacency." The company didn't listen. Their rationale was they had to write that sort of contract to retain the talent. The sales "talent" sold just three homes the next twelve months and was replaced by a husband and wife team who sold four homes the first month and six the second -- and continued on with a blazing sales pace .

There are no guarantees in life. Guarantees are opium to the masses of non producers looking for a free ride. In this case, the lady's expertise did not measure up to the size of her paycheck. In sales, the mantra is, "The greater the risk, the greater the reward!"

Deb

The Author of Reasons to Call Back

In today's world of selling homes, follow up is where the money is. Many sales people fail at follow up because they don't have a workable, organized database. This is rule number one. Today, the money is in the follow up.

In Maryland I encountered a salesperson who was a master at the follow up process. She was the author of the follow up program called, "Ten Reasons to Call Back." Her name was Deb. I first saw her making follow up calls during an evening phone-a-thon. Attached to her prospect file box and computer was a simple checklist entitled "Ten Reasons to Call Back." I watched Deb work from her checklist and saw she was very effective, calling back with a reason. From that, we developed the five rules of follow up:

1. Always have a reason for the call
2. Call the most sold husband or wife
3. Call with one-of-a-kind information
4. Call with urgency to come back
5. Close for the appointment

With Deb's permission, I expanded her ten reasons to call back into a forty reasons to call back flashcard which would be attached to the computer or prospect file box. Today, years later, sales people still use the 40 Reasons to Call Back checklist.

There is an interesting lesson for salespeople and sales management here. Deb was an accomplished accountant working in the back room. She saw the size of the commission checks going into the field. As a go-getter, she wanted some of that commission money for herself, so she prevailed upon management to let her take a sales position. Since she had no experience, they gave her the worst job in the company – a close out situation. With dispatch, Deb closed out the community and then asked for another community. They gave Deb the second worst job in the company and she sold that one out too. From that point forward, Deb's skills rewarded her with the best communities in the company from which she made the highest compensation. In the age before computers, she would take her prospect file box home every night and reconcile it daily. By reconciling, we mean moving the "Bs" to "As" and the "Cs" to "Bs" so she was always on top of her prioritization. Her large bank account was directly linked to her proficiency at follow up, reasonable closing skills, and a drive to make it all happen. She made moving from the back room to the front line look easy.

TOM TALKS... About Less is More

At the inauguration of the Gettysburg battlefield, the speaker that preceded Abraham Lincoln was the noted orator, Edward Everett. He proceeded to deliver what many contemporaries considered his finest speech. Then, the president rose and stunned the crowd with just two minutes of timeless eulogy. The president finished and the crowd sat in reverent silence. Edward Everett rushed up to Lincoln and said, "Mr. Lincoln, you distilled in two minutes what I could not communicate in over two hours!"

Aren't some sales presentations better shorter than longer? How about trying to put it all into a two-minute context for that next prospect who says, "Tell me what you've got here – and tell me fast!"

"Be sincere; be brief; be seated."

~Franklin D. Roosevelt

Mike

Telephone Discipline Pads the Wallet

We were doing a phone-a-thon one evening for a major corporation in Northern California. Their star salesperson was named Mike. We were told Mike had a world class follow up system and to observe him closely. Before the call out session started, Mike brought out his prospect cards and arranged them carefully on his desk top in descending order of importance – "A" first, "B" second, and "C" third. Then he picked up the phone receiver and put it to his ear. He did not stop calling until he had achieved five confirmed appointments for the ensuing seven day work week. That was about forty-five minutes into the exercise time frame. I complimented Mike on his achievement and then asked why he did not bring the telephone receiver down from his ear. I noticed that it was always rooted to his earlobe and never left. His answer was a classic, "I found out that if I am having a poor follow up evening, that receiver becomes heavier and heavier to pick up. Along about my fourth or fifth rejection, it becomes impossible to pick up. Very often I put it down and cancel the follow up calling for the evening. This way, I have a rule: never bring down the telephone until I have achieved one of two things – 1) Five confirmed appointments for the next seven day time frame, or 2) I have called the full time frame of one hour and fifteen minutes." I learned a great lesson from a master at follow-up.

TOM TALKS... About Teamwork

Several years ago there was a team of utility infielders that won lots of games in the Dallas market. No, these weren't baseball players. This was a husband and wife team that was passed around through the market as close out specialists. Builder A would use them to sell out a community and then refer them to his non competing friend, Builder B who would sell out his community and then refer the couple to Builder C. What was their secret?

The lady was wired into the local Board of Realtors. In fact, she was on the ethics committee. Her husband was a retired manufacturer salesperson who was a master closer. She generated the business - he closed at the site. It was a team made in heaven that helped several builders finish their communities in that market at that time.

Angelina

Word Painter Extraordinaire

You always remember the Medal of Honor presentations. Many, many years ago, I was on a LIFE magazine survey of the national market. Arriving at a community called Burton Hills in Nashville late in the day, I met an engaging sales professional. She insisted on escorting me over to her model park and as we paused in front of the homes, she asked if I saw something different about the brick construction.

"I sure do. It's highly detailed!"

She said, "I'm glad you saw that, because we build with commercial brick, not residential brick. Every brick that had to be sized correctly was cut with a brick saw, not hammered or lopped off by a trowel. This same attention to detail you will see magnified when you step inside and inspect our job built, hand rubbed, custom stained cabinetry. Come on, let's look at it."

She escorted me through an interior presentation that was the best of the best. This was a memorable use of words that I've remembered all these years. Not dissimilar to another presentation late in the afternoon in South Carolina where a builder named J.C. Roy was building replicas of Old Williamsburg. Here, the salesperson escorted me to a model home as the sun was dipping below the horizon. She said, "Shhh, listen, listen. Can you hear the pitter patter of horse's hoofs in the distance?"

I said, "Not really."

She said, "Listen again! Imagine it's late in the day in picturesque Williamsburg and here comes the old lamplighter riding his horse over cobblestones to light each and every gas lamp on this street?"

Wow, what a word picture. What a suggestion to the theater of my mind that I should own a home there. It was magnificent, and the presentation continued in kind. I wonder if salespersons spend enough time creating the engaging language and the compelling differentiations that come with the proper use of words. Words are the salesperson's tool that causes them to differentiate from the competition.

For example, which sounds better – "Is there anything that would prevent you from buying this home today?" Or,

"Is there anything that would keep us from moving forward right now?" You must agree the second phrase goes down easier than the first.

Let's remember, closing is like fine wine. It goes down smoothly and makes everybody feel good.

TOM TALKS... About a Medal of Honor Close

This is a wrap-up closing technique that allows you to ensure no obstacle to closure remains. Let's see how it works. You structure your presentation in a series of modules and close on each module making absolutely certain that you gain 100% agreement. Then, you move to the next module. For example, you close on **location** (wrap it up), close on **sense of community** (wrap it up), close on **background of the builder** (wrap it up), close on a **specific floor plan** (wrap it up), close on a **homesite uniqueness** (wrap it up), close on **financing** (wrap it up) and then test close for **one-of-a-kind**. If prospects say they have to sleep on it or think it over, you gently ease into the summary closing process by saying, "Let's review what you liked about it again, shall we?" Now, you review the benefits of the purchase. When you remind them, they've already agreed to each major benefit, the buyer should commit. If a sales coun<u>sell</u>or doesn't wrap up each module and therefore hears a rejection, where did the sale go awry? Wrap-up prevents this slippage and keeps the sale on track to completion.

Greta

The Power of Space Creation

The Hawaiian Islands are a great place to visit and a great venue to sell homes. Several years ago, there was a gorgeous beachfront community on the western edge of Oahu that was having difficulty selling. The reason was the Japanese buyer had come upon hard times and had vanished from the scene. The community was called Ko Olina. Furthermore, the architects had designed small spaces to accommodate small buyers. There were twenty-three attached residences of stacked flat condominiums left to sell. The existing sales team was maxed out. The Pacific Rim salesperson of the year, a professional named Greta, was assigned to this unique project.

The challenge in these designs was to create a feeling of space. We discovered that focusing on light sources made it possible to create more visual space depending where you stood in the floor plan. For example, if you stood at the front door and presented the property from the outside in, your eye hit the rear dining room wall and was drawn to the dark kitchen cabinetry and the space looked small. If you walked the prospects over to the dining room wall and looked over the dining area, through the kitchen and out to the balcony, and then into the living room and out through another window, the space magically looked larger. Greta, being a good soldier, worked hard at fine tuning her presentation according to the proper sequencing. After practicing with a tape recorder and doing numerous simulations, she finally got the presentation down pat. When her buyers arrived, she was an expert at creating space, looking through one light source to another. She knew where to take her buyers in the floor plans so, with them at her side, she could emphasize the feeling and flow of space. I called it a choreography of where to stand and what to look at in the "production" called selling style and design. The great composer Giuseppe Verdi did it too. He not only wrote the incredible music for his operas, he choreographed where the singers would stand during a performance.

Greta went on to complete the sales of that community in three and a half months. It was a testament to the expertise of a world class salesperson, hard work, and the utilization of a practiced coun<u>sell</u>ing process.

Wally

Enticing with Spices

If your presentation stalls and seems mired in the muck, ask this question, "What haven't I asked you that I should have asked you?"

It was one of those cold, blustery days in Denver, Colorado with the snow falling. I was shopping a mid range priced condominium community. It was the kind of cold that gnaws at your bones. Shuffling through the snow banks, I arrived at the entry to Wally's sales office. I opened the door and stepped into a cozy environment that reeked of a compelling aroma. Just then a salesperson bounded in front of me and introduced himself. "Hello, I'm Wally. Nice to have you here today. Come in and get yourself warm."

When I asked Wally what the aroma was he answered he was a collector of exotic teas. "This is an orange cinnamon tea from the Far East. Would you like a cup?"

Since I was freezing, I replied in the affirmative.

Wally concocted the most scalding cup of tea I've ever put to my lips which forced me to sit there for twenty minutes while he gave me his presentation. He was magnificent. It was couched in questions and anchored with U-benefits across the board. After the exposé of his product was finished, we entered the model home. If I had been a real buyer, I would have bought. Wally and I became friends and he shared with me that in truth he was not a collector of teas. He had devised this strategy to cause buyers to sit down longer and spend more time in the sales environment. He reasoned the more time he had with customers, the more opportunity he had to transfer knowledge and sell homes. It worked for him so it ought to work for other sales people.

TOM TALKS... About the Power of Scent

Many salespeople fail to seed their models with pleasing aromas. There are ways and means to do this like baking bread in an oven on big sales days. In Scotland, it's traditional to bring an armful of bread to a brand new resident. Bill in Canada does this with the loaves of bread he bakes on high traffic days. As you would expect, his referrals are high!

Dean

Selling Through Impossible Objections

Dean was one heck of a sales manager and sales professional. He came out of the sales development school that taught precisely what you do to bring a contract to conclusion. It was an October day and I was assigned to spend a few hours in his environment. I arrived at the job and found he was in the closing room attempting to write a contract. What helps the trainer is knowledge and selling style of the trainee. Unseen, I put my ear against the wall of the closing office and heard the wife of the buying unit say this, "Mr. Stewart, we are absolutely, positively not going to buy a home from you today."

This fact was conveyed with such conviction that I thought there was no way he could bring this couple to a decision at this time. There was a long pause. I wondered what was going on inside. Then I heard Dean speak to the husband. "Let me ask you sir. What do you like to do in your spare time?"

The husband said, "Play golf."

Dean said, "As I understand it, you've been looking for almost five months. Is that correct?"

The husband agreed.

"How's your golf game?" Dean asked.

"It's terrible!" was the answer.

Now, the husband was on Dean's side. Next I heard him speak to the wife, "Mrs. Jones, why don't you and your husband give your family the ultimate present for the holidays – a new home? I say this because at this stage of our construction, we can have that lovely home with the unobstructed view of the mountains completed in time. Imagine a brand new playroom for the kids, a workshop for dad, and a home theater! We can have all that finished by the holidays. Now," Dean continued, "pretend it's Christmas morning, you wake up early, come down the stairs, and discover your children are already enjoying their toys. Your son is playing with the electric train going around the tree and your daughter is cuddling the dolls hanging from the branches. You and Jimmy pinch each other and say, 'We've given our children the best Christmas they've ever had.' We can have you in by the holidays. It's all possible. Let's make it happen, shall we?"

There was a long, pregnant pause on the other side of that wall. You could cut the silence with a knife. I was wondering what would happen next. How would the lady wriggle out of this professional, low key call to action? Wriggle she did not. She said, "Mr. Stewart, you've opened my eyes to something. A Christmas present like a new home will be remembered forever by our kids." Then she spoke to her husband, "Dear, what do you think?"

Of course, Jimmy was on Dean's side. "I think it's a brilliant idea."

With that, the wife said to Dean, "What do we do next?"

In my book, that's a salesperson's dream – where they close you for the purchase, not the other way around!

That is a world class close by every definition imaginable. But, the best was yet to come! Not only did they move in their new home by Christmas, six weeks later, they brought a referral sale to this world class closer. A two for one is the best use of one's time – guaranteed!

The crux of this story is most sales people would have cratered with the 'absolutely, positively not going to buy' language. Does this deter the master closer? Absolutely not! The hallmark of the master closer is to <u>never</u>, <u>never</u>, <u>never</u> quit! With persistence Dean moved forward until he had secured the sale.

Vern

Never Rule Out the Impossible

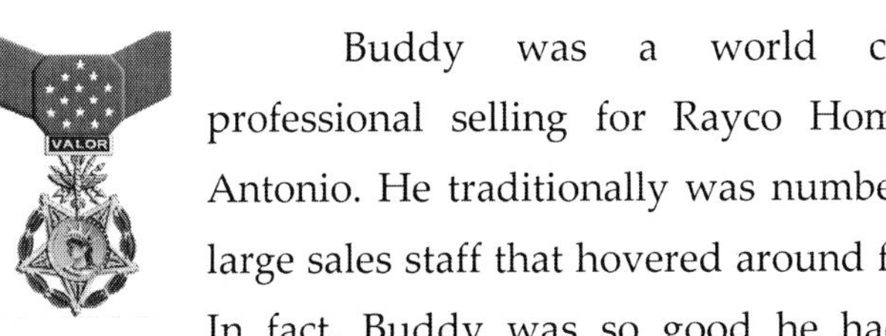

Buddy was a world class sales professional selling for Rayco Homes in San Antonio. He traditionally was number one on a large sales staff that hovered around fifty agents. In fact, Buddy was so good he had won the number one salesperson of the year award for three consecutive years. It was Buddy's fifth year of selling for the company and he was six sales ahead of his arch rival, Vern, with just three days left to the end of the year.

Buddy felt sure he had the company's No. 1 salesperson contest locked and pictured the $10,000 prize safely ensconced in his bank account. The only trouble was he didn't know Vern. With the contest seemingly safely won, Buddy took a skiing trip to Colorado. Vern saw his chance! Mustering all his follow up acumen, he called every possible prospect the next three days, told them he was in a life and death contest, and asked if they would buy from him this year instead of making the decision next year. As a sweetener, he gave his prospects the promise of additional time, effort, and a 24/7 commitment. Vern worked his phones from early morning until late at night and scored a super star's sales day.

Weldon, his sales manager told it like this:

"It was the afternoon of New Year's Eve and I was driving out to the project to console poor Vern on losing the contest to his arch rival, Buddy, another year. As I entered Vern's community, I was amazed to see a traffic jam of vehicles and a young framer directing traffic. As I entered the sales office, I noticed Vern's wife was in the corner helping with some paperwork while Vern was in the other corner writing a contract. Some of Vern's friends were providing holding action for the traffic. When I saw they were writing sales, I took off my coat and pitched in. We worked well into New Year's Eve until Vern had written ten solid contracts from his three day telephone follow up blitz. I've never seen anything like it!"

Here is an example of a salesperson who was determined not to be outsold for another year. He reached way deep – deep into his database – and came up with ten rock solid, fundable sales, all on the last day of the year. Now, that has to be a Medal of Honor presentation!

Story

49

Connie

Respecting and Honoring Construction

U.S. Home had a sales lady named Connie in Arizona that was so beloved by her construction crews, they would do anything for her. Connie had a big heart. On hot days she would bring them an ice bucket of cold drinks. On cold days, she would bring them steaming hot chocolate or coffee. She was always thinking of her construction people. She knew if they built a good home, she would have great sales!

The company ran a major year end contest and as bad luck would have it, Connie was well behind on what needed to be accomplished to win the contest. This competition was based on closed or funded sales, not originated sales. They had to be completed and funded on time for her to be eligible for a company sponsored trip to the Bahaman islands. She had done all she could do on the selling end, now it was up to her construction crews. Because she was so respected by her trade partners and construction workers, the whole construction team worked overtime, some without additional pay, to get the number of homes closed she required. In fact, they worked Saturdays and Sundays from very early in the morning until very late at night until the construction team was absolutely certain she had made the cut. When Connie came back from her well earned trip, guess what she did? She hosted a gigantic barbecue for the construction team, complete with the very best catered vittles and a mariachi band. What an inspiring example of team effort between construction and sales.

TOM TALKS... About What Makes a Salesperson Successful

Having a Healthy Ego Drive: This trait marries ego strength with competitiveness and produces that all-encompassing desire to persuade people to buy and close the sale.

Having Empathy: This is the ability to balance ego drive with the capacity to place oneself in someone else's shoes. An incredibly important trait when you're closing, pressure reducing, closing, pressure reducing, as in the professional closing presentation!

Michelle

Going the Extra Mile

Michelle was one of the very best sales agents in the mid-West. She knew the importance of proper staging and the critical nature of the tour. When Michelle took her "guests" on a driving journey through her community, she always sat the wife in the right front seat and the husband in the right rear. Why? So she had easy contact with the decision maker – normally the woman – and with just a cock of the head she had eye contact with the husband in the right rear. Something else! She always carried a mounted community map which was given to the lady as the property was toured. The map was mounted on light foam board so it wouldn't crease, crinkle, or fold over when it was opened up. The wife would scan the map for the exact location in the community and then hand the map to her husband in the back seat. This simple tool was so effective it became standard equipment in that builder's selling tool box.

Michelle was a master at walking on the homesite with her eight cones and a complete complement of tools to make that building site come alive. As Michelle put it, "When you see bright red cones on a homesite – in each site corner and each pad corner, it gives a whole other dimension to the property. It causes the spread to look large and inviting."

Finally, Michelle was known to take digital pictures on her tour which were e-mailed to the prospects as a potent follow up tool. Master closers go the extra mile.

TOM TALKS... About Sales Success Tenets

Making the grade in a tough, competitive market isn't easy. Ask the new home salesperson in Monterrey, Mexico who sold a home in a market when interest was 55%. He was truly a master closer!

The Sales Pros who are making it happen exercise three tenets for success:

1. Discover the buyers in depth and spend quality time. Sell with a positive mental attitude.
2. Sell to a process. It's called connection coun<u>sell</u>ing, and it embraces all the selling steps leading up to the close. Ask questions! Ask questions!
3. Sell with persistence. Don't give up. Come to closure with a one-of-a-kind!

Caroline

Financing is Key

"Sweet Caroline," as the words of the song say, was all sweetness and light when it came to working with her customers. Behind the scenes, she was a driven, world class closer. The secret to her success was she had experience in two seemingly diverse fields yet, they were surprisingly helpful in closing sales. She had eleven years experience in the mortgage brokerage business and six years of experience with the Internal Revenue Service. If anyone doubts whether you sell and close homes with your financing, they should have watched Caroline in action. She was a whiz at synergizing her financing knowledge with her federal tax knowledge. When she calculated an after tax cost of housing number, you knew it was correct right down to the last decimal. When she did an alternate of choice presentation on which mortgage was best for the subject family, it was right on the money. Watching her in action would convince anyone that financing is at least one-third if not more of the purchasing proposition.

TOM TALKS... About Listening

No sales book should be written today without alluding to the power of listening. Most sales people talk 80% of the time and ask questions or listen only 20% of the time. This is fact. Turn that around to a three to one rule where the salesperson asks questions and listens 75% of the time and talks only 25% of the time, or, a simple 50/50 rule. Ask one question for every one piece of information you give.

The power of listening tells the sales professional exactly where she or he is in the presentation. The customer will tell you, but you have to ask. The power of listening can move toward a close. Such as, "Based on what you shared with me, we've found a floor plan that works. Is that correct?" Or the power of listening will be essential when asking the closing question. "Since this home contains what you said you were looking for, let's make it yours, shall we?" It's a shame how many sales people step on customer's lines or talk right through a close. The master closer understands that we are born with two ears and one mouth which simply means listen twice as much as you talk. If we would put this practice into play, the housing industry would boom and accelerate the comeback of our economy.

Joan

Ice Cream and a Half Million Dollars

Here is a Medal of Honor presentation par excellence. It was northern Virginia back in the days when the market was really in the tank. Homes were not selling. It was the '73-'74 recession and everyone was scrambling for traffic. The sales lady, Joan, told the story beautifully. Let's recall her words.

"It was a slow Monday afternoon after a non eventful weekend. I looked out my window and saw this white Good Humor truck drive into my neighborhood and stop at the playground. The ice cream salesman got out in a white uniform and proceeded to kick a football high in the air. Every little kid that caught the football got an ice cream stick, but something strange was happening. The child did not have to pay for the ice cream. Tuesday afternoon, the same thing happened. In rolled the ice cream truck, out came the

Good Humor man, up went the football, and every kid who caught the football got a free ice cream stick. Same thing on Wednesday. When the ice cream truck pulled into my community on Thursday, my curiosity got the better of me. I went outside, walked up to the ice cream salesman and asked, 'Sir, do you mind if I ask you a question? I've been watching you for three days. You kick a football in the air. A child catches it and they get free ice cream. How can you afford to do this?'

"The ice cream salesman said, 'You see it's like this. I'm fulfilling a fantasy. I just sold a large corporation and I'm chilling out after many years of hard work. I've always wanted to be an ice cream salesman. And, I'm having a great time giving these kids free ice cream.'"

Now the alert sales lady snapped to attention and asked, "Sir, have you thought about purchasing a new home?"

The answer came back, "My wife and I are looking as we speak."

The sales lady booked an appointment for the ice cream salesman, sans uniform, and his wife to tour her community. She sold them a half million dollar home in a down market. Tell me sales people don't make the difference! They do!

"Opportunities multiply as they are seized."
~Sun Tzu

Sally

Thinking Outside the Orange

There was a heck of an Orange Julius vender in Southern California who marketed to employees of the giant TRW Systems Company. He sold his Orange Julius drinks from a small, nondescript soft drink stand right at the entrance and exit to the plant. Sally, an enterprising new home salesperson, thought since he was right in the main stream of traffic when the shift workers entered or left the plant, what a great place to put her brochures. So, she visited the Orange Julius man and asked if he would put her brochures on his counter and motivate people to visit her homes. She would stamp his and her names on the brochures and reward him when a sale was made. What kind of reward would make him happy?

The Orange Julius man thought for a moment and then said, "Well, don't tell my wife, but from time to time I like to take a little nip of Vodka with my Orange Julius."

So, Sally, the prospecting pro, said that every time a prospect arrived with her brochure in hand and they bought a home, she would bring over a bottle of Vodka. "What's your favorite brand?"

"Smirnoff" was the answer.

Now Sally said, "I won't bring you just a fifth of vodka, I'll bring you a half gallon. How does that sound?"

"That's the best deal I've heard all day," and the motivated Orange Julius man went to work.

A year later, the Orange Julius stand had generated fourteen sales to that enterprising sales professional and she had reciprocated with fourteen half gallons of Vodka! Rumor has it the Orange Julius man was the happiest vender in Southern California.

Story

54

Virginia

Farming the Chamber of Commerce

Virginia was a prospecting maven. She knew that the Chamber of Commerce in Fort Worth was actively soliciting queries from companies transferring into the area. So, she went to the head of the Chamber and asked if she could have access to their lead list. She got it and proceeded to send out brochures and make follow up phone calls to every query on the list. A year later, Virginia had scored six high end home sales. It was an impressive volume for its time and taught Virginia and the balance of her sales team this important lesson. Plug into other lead gathering sources and you may find interest in purchasing a home.

"To do prospecting right, ask everyone in sight!"

~Tom Richey

Cynthia

The Smart Discretionary

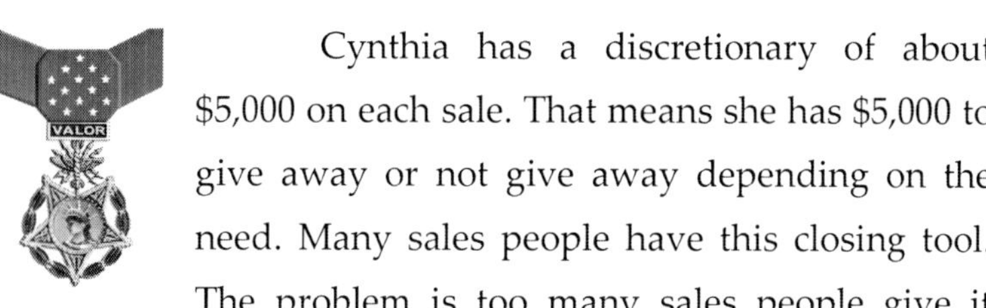

Cynthia has a discretionary of about $5,000 on each sale. That means she has $5,000 to give away or not give away depending on the need. Many sales people have this closing tool. The problem is too many sales people give it away needlessly. It doesn't have to be that way. Cynthia uses her discretionary like this. First, she understands that if Smith gets something Jones doesn't, it could create ill will among her home owners. Sooner or later, Smith and Jones will chat with each other and if one has a marked advantage, that will work against her referrals. So, Cynthia sells from a level playing field, but she does it like this.

She does not give away the discretionary to close the sale. However, several days later she calls her buyers and says, "By the way, I have good news for you. The day you purchased, I was empowered to offer you a $5,000 shopping spree or payment of closing costs, or help with your financing, and I want to make sure you receive that. So, in order to work it into your purchase, which would you prefer?"

Her referral sales are extraordinarily high. The fact she does something that nobody does contributes to that high rate big time! When a home buyer makes a deal and then the deal is changed to their benefit later, it becomes great fodder for conversations that promote the salesperson and the builder.

TOM TALKS... About Nobody Walking!

Lester Goodman one of the true gurus of new construction marketing, has this suggestion for today's tough market. When traffic visits your store, NOBODY WALKS! That's right, Les says nobody walks! What he means is nobody leaves without a best effort, full blown presentation, arriving as close to a one-of-a-kind and contract signing as possible. The "Nobody walks!" philosophy will sell more homes over the course of a year.

"Footprints in the housing sands of time were not made by folks who stood still."

~Tom Richey

J.J.

First One Remembered

J.J. Gallahar was the NAHB Salesman of the Year for Ryland Homes. One evening I'm at a friend's home and the phone rings at 9:15 pm. The husband picks up the telephone and says, "J.J., what in the world are you doing calling me at this hour?"

The question was asked in good spirits, so I rushed over to the phone and said, "J.J. what are you doing making a phone call at this time on a Sunday evening?"

J.J. remonstrated me with, "The last one talked to is the first one remembered." He always called his top ten prospects Sunday evening to remind them of good old J.J. and the fact that he would be contacting them to come back again. And, oh yes. He proudly hung his 'Salesman of the

Year' plaque squarely behind his desk in the closing zone. "Buyer's want to buy from winners, not losers," he often said.

TOM TALKS... About Personal Motivation

Selling is a lonely world. Very often home sales people whether new or resale, work in a world of self-doubt, lack of information, rude customers, demanding bosses, and a time frame that isn't always conducive to consistent earnings. So, they have to be continually motivated. The great sales professionals, sales managers, and coaches know this as do the great champions of business. In fact, John Madden, coach of the Oakland Raiders and renowned TV football analyst told me the year he won the Super Bowl, he made the point of talking to his primary players at least once a day. His talk was not about conditioning, the playbook, or the next game. Nor was it a casual chat about the lifestyles of the rich and famous. It was a down home friendly talk about how the kids were doing in school, or how construction on the new home was coming, or about the new arrival. In short, it was just something of interest to relax the player and meld the players as a team. Madden was a master at bringing discipline to bear in a casual way, not a bombastic way. Although, bottom line, he was the supreme disciplinarian, his methods worked!

Every salesperson and every sales manager should talk to themselves every day in positive terms. One might ask, "Am I going up or going down the production curve?" Or, "Today is the first day of the rest of my life." Or, "Yesterday is a canceled check, today is legal tender, and tomorrow is a promissory note." Self motivation works wonders.

Quint

Bulldog Persistence

Sales people need to say to themselves every day of their life, "It's a beautiful day and I'm going to improve someone's lifestyle." Could there be a better mission in life than to sell the American Dream? In this market of ravaged real estate, negative media, and confused consumers, home sales people need to be the guiding light. They need to be that one inspirational voice that leads people toward the right decision while never pushing them into it. Sales managers need to understand that they get better when their sales staff gets better. The salesperson is the customer of the sales manager/coach. The home buyer is the customer of the salesperson. Each layer has to do it's very best to cause positive, not negative events to happen. A negative happens when a family refuses to purchase a home and leaves their buying power on the sideline. The economy suffers, the job market falters, and the challenges multiply. When a salesperson sells a cut above and a step ahead and truly communicates the benefit of buying now, not later, a positive force happens, a sale is made, and the economy prospers.

A young salesperson named Quint shared with me this metaphor. He and his wife went to Mexico for their anniversary. While on vacation, they visited a zoo. One of the main attractions at the zoo was the lions. After finally finding where they were located, they were thoroughly unimpressed. These lions were grossly overweight and they pitied them because these former kings of the jungle had morphed into overweight, lethargic, and helpless spectacles. These lions were fed high caloric meals on a platter every day and were losing their natural instincts. What would happen if they were thrown back into the jungle? Would they even survive? After returning to the States, Quint made the connection that being in the home sales business between the years of 2000 and 2006 was similar to the situation of the lions in the zoo. Realtors and builder reps were fed a steady stream of buyers and it seemed as though it would be that way forever. Like the lions, many became lethargic and overweight with self-pride, while at the same time the natural instincts and selling skills atrophied. This is where the comparison ends because unlike the lions at the zoo, in 2007 we *were* thrown back into the jungle. The free lunch was over. Those that wandered aimlessly in the jungle waiting for their broker or builder to funnel them buyers on a platter became disillusioned and many perished. Those that are still in the professional home sales business today have gone through a very challenging, humbling, and exhilarating experience. Challenging in that we have had to be self-starters and self-motivators. Humbling in that we have had to shed years of self pride and humble ourselves by going back to the basics. That means being willing to go to any lengths to relearn the basics of selling, prospecting, and follow up. Exhilarating because deep down inside, *every true sales professional loves a good hunt!* Whether the market gets better or not, we, as sales professionals, can always get better!

We, like lions in the jungle, have to scavenge for food and be strong and alert for potential competitors. We have to understand that today we are at war. This is not fun and games. This economy is based on survival of the fittest. Therefore, the jungle analogy is dead on. The important point is, let's stop underestimating our abilities and capacities and emphasize our positives. Let's look at the glass as half full, not half empty. Let's remember what Ralph Waldo Emerson said, "Enthusiasm, if you have it, thank God for it – if you don't have it, get down on your knees and pray for it." Let's remember that enthusiasm moves mountains. If you truly believe and truly communicate the benefits of a new home purchase, sales will happen. We must remember we have the lowest rates in thirty years, we have pent up demand, we have available product, and all we have to do is sell through the home buyer's negativity. Not an easy job, but one the master closer, the lion in the jungle, will accomplish with positive mental attitude.

The bottom line is what do we have inside of us? In football it's called heart. In the military it's called heroism. In life it's called character. In home selling, it's called passion and persistence – bulldog persistence.

TOM TALKS... About Tough Closes

One Sales Pro, when reflecting on how he closed a tough one, said he had the family ready to write, but couldn't ease them over the line. They wanted to wait until Tuesday. The buyers said they were "rock solid and would buy for sure." The Sales Pro had heard that before, so he gently nudged with the phrase, "Do you really want to wait until next Tuesday? How would you feel if someone else's name went on your property between now and then?" (Pause) Then, after an appropriate silence, the buyers said, "We'd feel like we'd missed an opportunity," and they bought. The subtleties of professional coun<u>sell</u>ing score big!

"Vision without action is only a dream.
Action without vision is wasting time.
Vision and action can change the world!"
~Confucious

Denny, Bill, & Sue

Selling Over, Around, and Through

Denny was a great salesperson. At the height of the '73-'74 recession when I was traveling to Washington a great deal, he said, "Go on up there to Washington, and tell them to prolong the recession. I'm having the best year I've ever had."

I've often wondered if recessions are manufactured in one's mind. Take my friend Bill Watson. He confirmed that in one month this year, he will take home commission checks of over $80,000 at a time when other people are joining 'whine and sleaze' parties. Or, the former NAHB's National Sales & Marketing Council Salesperson of the Year, Sue Miller, who when asked at her award ceremony why she had such an outstanding year answered, "I felt I could sell over, sell around, and sell through any objection I heard." The interesting thing about this comment was years before I was talking to the great football running back, Jim Brown, and asked him a similar question. "Jim, what made you a legend in your own time?" The great football icon said, "I felt I could run through, run around, or run over anyone who got in my way."

Great performers think in similar ways.

TOM TALKS... About Expectations

We were helping a major corporation hire a sales staff in Phoenix one day when an obviously well heeled, well blinged lady sashayed in for the interview. She plopped down in an oversized chair and calmly said, "Mr. Garrett (the sales manager), I want you to know I have to make at least $100,000 a year or I won't take this job." Now, I was not supposed to verbally partake in the interview process but I couldn't help myself.

"Young lady," I said, "Surely you must know only the federal government makes money. The rest of us have to earn it."

She didn't get the message and continued her plea for easy pay and was shown the door after a few minutes. The point here is when a salesperson combines Energy, Expertise, and Efficiency (the Vitamin E's) into their sales presentations, good things happen – mainly a large paycheck!

"Expectations are not bankable until they become realizations!" *~Tom Richey*

15 Effective Follow Up Procedures

1. You must always have a **reason** for calling.
2. Always set a **specific** date and time for your appointment.
3. Confirm the appointment with an **e-mail**, a **letter** or a card.
4. Make a **reminder phone call.**
5. Flag the **appointment date and time** in your time management system.
6. Don't shoot all your **selling ammunition** on the first go-round. Leave something in reserve for a reason to come back.
7. Always get on a **first name** basis.
8. Call your **best rapport** prospect for the re-appointment. Get cell phone and work numbers!
9. Ascertain the **dominant buying motive** and roadblock to the sale. Follow up to the buyer's agenda.
10. Keep accurate **follow up** records.
11. Tie in strong measures of **urgency**.
12. Be **enthusiastic!**
13. Set all your be-back appointments for **convenience hours.**
14. Use the '**which close**' to nail down the appointment.
15. Be **consistent** with your follow up!

Larry

Mastering the Open Ended Question

Larry was an incredible new home sales professional who was far ahead of his time. He believed purchasing a home was a private affair that could not be rushed with phony process or invalid scenarios. These were the days when salespersons were trained to sell in straight jacket fashion by memorizing a sequence of selling checkpoints and then not departing from them. It was brutal and ill advised. Some called it the Critical Path but it was no such thing. It was simply a canned pitch that stifled the salesperson's creativity and misdirected the purchaser's decision.

Larry would sit his prospects in a totally relaxing atmosphere and invite them to discuss their new home dreams. He was a master of the open ended question, "Tell me about the home in your future. Let's see how close we can come to your dream." Larry knew the power of one-of-a-kind and plugged into its closing power. However, he readily knew the ultimate goal would be reached through intense listening and the continual use of questions. I once heard him say, "Please go home and think about this. I'm not going to ask you to commit today. We want to be totally comfortable with this decision, don't we?" And, of course, the family almost begged Larry to take their check. A master of the reverse sell he was! A proponent of high pressure he was not! Larry would say, "If you ask the right kind of questions and listen carefully, your friends will tell you what kind of home to sell them – and at what price and terms."

I wanted Larry to enter the National Sales and Marketing Council's Salesperson of the Year award. He refused, so I entered for him. He won and his acceptance speech was a classic. He credited home sales for helping him establish a mission in a third world country, put five kids through college, and help the building fund of his local church construct a magnificent new house of worship.

When you add up all the happy families the "Larrys" in our country create by selling the American dream, and when you fathom the richness of the experience selling new or resale homes, isn't selling homes an incredibly rewarding experience? Ask Larry Lamb.

"Sell the product on your feet, close with financing in your seat."

~Tom Richey

Story

60

Clark

The Share-With-Me Kid

Winchester Homes trained a young salesperson named Clark to peak proficiency by focusing on asking questions. "Ask more questions than you give out information," they admonished, and it became his selling style. Clark drilled, practiced, and rehearsed in the "share with me" mode.

"Share with me what's important to you and we'll build your dream home together."

"Share with me what you have in mind?"

"Share with me what's the most important room in your next home."

"Share with me who's the chef in the family and what's your specialty?"

"Share with me if there are any special hobbies or passions we need to be aware of like art collecting, music, physical fitness, or sports on television for example?"

"Share with me what you like or would like to change about your present home?"

"Share with me what your budget is for monthly payments?"

"Share with me, do you entertain formally or informally?"

"Share with me how many people would be living in this home?"

These and other "share with me's" caused Clark to earn the nickname, 'The Share-With-Me-Kid.' He was a master at the non threatening probe and it showed in his consistently large paycheck.

You read it here. *The* home selling of the future is question-based selling. We call it question-driven counselling. It's comforting, participating, revealing, bond building, and best of all, it greases the track to the close. Rudyard Kipling had it right in his verse from *Elephant Child…*

"I keep six honest serving men.

They taught me all I knew.

Their names are What and Why and When

And How and Where and Who."

Janice

No Closing Equals No Sales

Years ago in the southeastern market, there was a company called Equity Homes. There was a sales lady on staff named Janice who, they felt, had extraordinary potential. They asked me to invest countless hours role playing the closing process with her. We role played … we drilled … we practiced … we rehearsed. However, Janice would not or could not get a grasp on this critical selling tenet. A closer she was not! Finally, after a great deal of effort, she confided in me she did not purchase her own goods and services the way we taught. In other words, she would never "succumb to a closing process." She would never be mesmerized or anesthetized by a "master closer." She would buy on her own cognition and only after a long period of shopping and comparison. She would not be "pushed," as she called it, into a sale. With effort, patience, and practice after practice, we tried to show her that closing sales was not pushiness, manipulation, or high pressure. It was the logical and emotional result of a salesperson's professional presentation. She didn't buy it! As a consequence, she drifted from company to company in her quest for success. She blamed her lack of production on four conditions: 1) unqualified traffic, 2) poor product, 3) no urgency, and 4) buyers are liars! After all, "Janice was trying real hard."

Twenty-two years later, I was working in the Northern California market when Janice appeared. She had worked her way west with failure after failure. During the interim, she had drifted from countless companies and had never realized her goal of a reasonable income. She finally made it to the coast and lasted with my client just a few weeks. The bottom line was that Janice would not buy into the closing process. She did not understand that if you don't ask, you don't get! And, you don't sell the way you buy!

How many "Janices" in the world are there who fail in real estate sales because they over intellectualize the closing process. Just step up and close, my friend. Step up and close! Janice failed because she suffered from a disease called 'Closing Avoidance.' If you don't buy into the closing ethic, you'll die from mal-compensation!

"Research shows that 80% of all sales are made after the 5th close. Most salespeople know three closes and use two." ~Tom Richey

Manny

The Magic Space Creator

We were in Tucson, Arizona training a twenty person sales staff with the Estes Company. The new land plan showed that the depth of the homesites had been shortened. As we went through a model demo, we segued to the leisure side or the backyard of the home where the sales staff was dismayed to see the depth of the sites. I don't know what prompted us to do this, but for some reason I suggested we walk to the back property line, turn around and look from the back of the property line to the back of the model to see if we could gain a different perspective or enlarge the space. Magically, the homesite appeared to open up to a one-third larger size. Then we took the staff to the corners and looking from that oblique angle we also enjoyed a larger visual size.

We went to a vacant homesite and looked from the back of the property to the front and it looked a great deal larger than looking from the front to the back. We implemented the mandate that everybody that came through for a presentation was taken to the leisure side property line, turned around, with the point made that there was more than enough space for family activities in the rear yards. It convinced the sales staff and the homes were sold.

Curious about this, I took that process to a space psychologist who verified that in some situations spaces will look larger than others. He verified that if you want that yard to look larger, you do exactly what we stumbled upon – take customers to the rear property line where it will appear to be one-third larger!

When we go to Mexico and work with the mini sized houses where the rear property lines are several steps away from rear façade, it still works. It works with condominium balconies, townhouse patios, small yards of any kind, or a giant yard where you want it to be larger.

Being aware that little things sell homes can make a major difference in your presentation and your income. This part of the home selling process is called urgency detailing.

The star salesperson, Manny, took the rear yard demo as his own. On every presentation he insisted the buyers walk to the rear property line, turn around, and observe the heightened space. Manny was on fire! He loved this demo and it worked for him. He soared to the Number one position on this large sales staff.

TOM TALKS... About Practice, Practice, Practice

Being a guitar aficionado, I was interested in Andreas Segovia's comment about practice. "If I don't practice for one day, I know it. If I don't practice for two days, my audience knows it."

Peppi Romero, the great guitar impresario came to Houston. I wanted to ask him one question. After the admirers subsided and all his tapes and CDs were sold, I was the last one in line. "Mr. Romero," I asked, "You are known as one of the premier guitarists in the whole world. I have one question. How often do you practice?" This master of the guitar answered without hesitation.

"Well, of course, I practice seven days a week anywhere from five hours on the off day to eight hours on a regular day. So, I say it's an average of about seven hours a day, 24/7."

I was literally blown away. I had heard Frank Sinatra had started and stopped his song, "My Way," several hundred times and that Benny Goodman used to practice his clarinet multiple hours every day, but I never dreamed a world class icon at his level of accomplishment would still devote that much time to practice. When you look at the great ones, it's obvious that according to the words of Vince Lombardi, "Perfect practice makes perfect."

Story

63

David & Nikki

Financing Knowledge Saves the Day

Here is a word-for-word account of a super tough financing-driven sale by master closer, David Bonnsman.

"Nikki is a single mother of three children, ages 2, 5 and 7. She works as a shift manager at a fast food chain earning roughly $34,000 per year. She receives no child support. She is a first time homebuyer, had very poor credit and had little or no money set aside for down payment or closing costs and had no immediate family in a position to help. She lived in a small, 2 bedroom, 1 bath apartment paying approx $800/month.

"When Nikki first came in my model home, there was no question about her desire to purchase, but her ability to purchase based on her situation was difficult to say the least. The townhomes I was selling were arguably the best value of any new construction in SW Wyoming. Very large, 1,700+ sq. ft., three large bedrooms with big closets, 2½ baths, oversized two-car garage located in a beautiful maintenance free community priced in the mid $170's. Compared to her current living situation, these townhomes represented a significant move-up in lifestyle for Nikki and her family.

"After her initial visit we set a follow-up appointment to complete a sales agreement, which was written three months ago. According to FHA guidelines (31% front end ratio) Nikki would not qualify for traditional financing, however, at the time I had a finance option through WCDA (Wyoming Community Development Authority), 100% financing (zero down) with a step-down subsidized interest rate of 3.5% (no monthly MI), which allowed Nikki to qualify for a payment slightly under $900/month.

"Feeling good about Nikki's ability to qualify for a mortgage through WCDA we started working on her credit with mid-score in the 560 range with multiple collections/late pays but thankfully no bankruptcy, repossessions or judgments to deal with. We enrolled Nikki with NitroCredit, credit repair specialists, and they went to work. Nikki was advised to open several secured trade lines of credit, while Nitro disputed and successfully fixed 29 of 33 disputed items raising her scores above the minimum 620.

"During the credit repair process an unexpected event took place. The WCDA 3.5% finance program ran out of funding and was eliminated (not to be replaced). After several unsuccessful lobbying attempts with the WCDA staff including the executive director, we started a letter writing campaign which included our local congressman and the Governor of Wyoming. The letter campaign resulted in several sympathetic responses, but since WCDA is set up as a quasi-government, self run agency, there was little or nothing they could do to assist.

"I then contacted a lender I previously worked with, that I knew was creative in working through difficult situations. I outlined Nikki's situation to Lennette of Mountainside Mortgage and she found a 5/1 FHA ARM with a 4.125% rate and a program that allowed Nikki to use the $8,000 first time homebuyer tax credit for the required 3.5% down payment. This seemed like a workable program, with a payment slightly higher than she wanted, but a payment that she could manage, so we kept the process moving forward.

"While working through Nikki's situation, I had started working with another buyer with an unrelated set of challenges that lead me to USDA, Section 502 Direct Loans. After researching and consulting with the Riverton, WY branch office about their low income targeted direct loans, I advised Nikki to submit an application for this program. I am happy to convey that Nikki was approved for a 3% USDA subsidized loan with a resulting $800/month payment on her new home.

"It was a hard fought battle, but the sheer joy of her family made the effort more than worthwhile. Every deal in today's real estate market seems to have its own unique set of challenges. How easy it is to write them off and wait for the easy one to walk through your door. But, where is the fun in that?"

Way to go, David!

TOM TALKS... About a Compromise Close

This close works best when it is executed at the very end of the presentation. Some Sales pros call it "the hand on the door knob of the car" close. You reach a point where the decision to purchase is stalled and then you say, "If I can secure an approval to your request, will you O.K. this agreement right now?"

In other words, you communicate that you are going to compromise, if they will be reasonable and execute the agreement.

Or, here's another version: "To be fair, let's meet halfway on this. If I can get an approval on one-half of what you are asking, will you go ahead and tie this property up today?"

This close appeals to the sporting instinct and is often all the tough negotiator needs to justify the purchase.

Please note that the compromise does not embrace a price reduction. The builder's home is a fair traded item and should not be subjected to random discounting.

Story

64

Jack

Selling a Shrine

The Asian couple looked disappointed. They told their salesperson, Jack, they had to have a home in Jack's price range that had an extraordinarily large dining area. The problem was no competing plans had that and no builder would customize. Since Jack's plan had an expansive dining area adjacent to a great room, the couple wondered if Jack's builder would eliminate the wall separating the two spaces. If so, they would buy the home.

Jack went to his builder who said, "You know, Jack, we are not a custom builder. We don't move walls. However, that is not a bearing wall so if you can get enough cash beyond the required down payment, we would entertain the idea."

Jack went back to his buyers wondering why this space was so important. He explained the reason for the additional cash and the fact they were stretching company policy. Since the wall change was not a major construction feat, they would do it, but they needed to put down cash outside the contract. The buyers were delirious. They wrote a check for the additional cash, and the contract was signed, sealed, and deal-ivered.

Jack's curiosity got the better of him. After the buyers had been in their home thirty days, Jack knocked on the door with a house warming gift. When he was ushered inside, his jaw dropped. In the enlarged dining-living space was a magnificent Buddhist shrine – the likes of which you would see in Myanmar. It was splendid! It was monumental. It was a cultural masterpiece! The best was yet to come. The Asian family got so many compliments from their friends, they referred two sales because of the extra effort by Jack and the builder.

TOM TALKS... About What Makes a Salesperson Successful

Being Skeptical: Today's new buyer has fostered a healthy sense of suspicion or disbelief in what they do or say. This keeps top salespeople alert and in the questioning and tie-down mode. Great salespeople look for meta, or truthful messages.

The Capacity to Sell Lifestyle: The ability to comprehend concepts and ideas and translate them for the buyer is critical to the complex coun<u>sell</u>ing or lifestyle selling of today.

The Oracle of Delphi

What Did He Say?

A Medal of Honor commendation should be given to the salespeople of antiquity who created the Oracle of Delphi. The Oracle was established as a revenue producer. Whenever Greek citizens had a question of import, they would seek the advice of the great Oracle and pay a fee. The Oracle quickly learned that to keep his customers satisfied, he had to give answers the customers wanted to hear – in a manner that obfuscated their meaning.

A young soldier was going to the Persian wars. He wanted to know if he would return home alive or be killed in conflict. He trundled off from his village, hiked over the hills and into the valleys until he reached the coastal plain and the great Oracle. As he entered, there was an ear splitting clang of cymbals, a roll of drums, a cacophony of bugles, and flashing fires. The Oracle was well merchandized!

At the precise moment, the Oracle said, "Oh, youthful soldier, what is your request?"

"Oh, great Oracle," the young soldier said. "I am going off to the Persian wars. Will I return alive?"

The Oracle answered in an agonizingly slow and commanding voice, "You shall return not fall in war."

The young soldier interpreted this to mean he would be spared in the conflicts and return home alive. He sprinted back to his village. With excitement he told everyone he would be spared until he met his language professor who said, "Young man, where did the great Oracle put the comma?"

The soldier replied, "What do you mean?"

The teacher said, "If the Oracle responded 'You shall return, not fall in war,' you will be saved. If the Oracle said, 'You shall return not, fall in war' you will be killed. Which is it?"

The young soldier answered what he wanted to believe the Oracle's answer was, "I shall not fall in war."

Today, salespeople should not tell buyers what they want to hear. They should tell it like it is. The moral of this story is that salespeople must be precise in their language and emphasis on words and phrases. In short, are we communicating succinctly what we want to say? This can be done through your choice of words and voice inflection. For example, take the word 'Whataburger.'

You can say, "What, a burger? I ordered a hot dog!"

Or, you can say, "What a burger! This is terrific."

Or, you can say, "What a burger" in a tone that implies an unappetizing meal.

So, it's not only the right choice of words, it's the right voice inflection that makes for sound sales communication!

TOM TALKS... About Value Footage

Here's the argument for an involved model home demonstration: Sherlock Holmes said, "We see but we don't observe." Many potential home buyers self-tour themselves through a model home to judge whether the floor plan works, the light sourcing is adequate, the finish and trim is as expected, or the spaces are as required. Potential home buyers are not trained to look for hidden sales points such as raised ceilings, additional light sources, value footage - not square footage, traffic patterns with no dead areas - and a host of other urgency details *i.e.,* details that would cause buyers to buy. What in the world does square footage mean? One could build a home two feet wide and a thousand feet long. It would have two thousand square feet, but a human being couldn't live in it - only a snake. Value footage is defined as footage that contributes to the lifestyle of the owner. Every square inch of space works and there are no dead ends or wasted hall space. Properly demonstrated, buyers will recognize value footage in a heartbeat and reject plain old vanilla square footage.

Nancy

Canvassing – The Tough Sell

We were marketing a resort community on the Gulf coast called Tennison. A logical market to generate traffic was New Orleans. We enlisted Nancy as our lead OPC prospect generator. OPC stands for Off Premise Canvassing – arguably the toughest type of selling. By definition, it is walking the streets of a tourist area, tapping people on the shoulder, and asking them if they would like to attend a breakfast or lunch about a spectacular real estate opportunity. It is a taxing business and not for the faint of heart. Nancy was strong! She was one of those magnificent human beings who says, "Show me what to do, Boss, and I'll make it happen."

With appropriate training, we put Nancy on the street to ingratiate, demonstrate, and consummate potential buyers into a presentation at a local hotel. The buyers were given the pitch and expected to buy right then and there. Perhaps the purest form of selling is off premise canvassing with a close for property off site. Millions of dollars of property and time shares are still sold in this manner. Nancy was a great student and a great practitioner. She would fearlessly introduce herself to strollers and invite them to look at an attractive brochure. She would schedule a breakfast and introduce them to the master closers who went into their spiel and closed quite a few properties.

When a salesperson says he or she does not have enough traffic, I wonder if we could implant a little bit of "Nancy" into their physical being. In other words, if the business doesn't come to you as a professional salesperson, you go to where the business is. It's called generating your own business. "When all else fails, go offsite."

"Are you in earnest? Seize this very minute! Boldness has genius, power, and magic in it. Only engage, and then the mind grows heated. Begin, and then the work will be completed."

~Jean Anouilh

Neal

No Nonsense Discovery

Neal Olive is one heck of a salesperson for Breland Homes. He is the consummate networker. In Neal's database, which goes back several years, he has copious records on family profiles, passions, hobbies, children, work, and a myriad of insights that a true lover of people would glean. Neal has been known to write sales two and three years into the database and make many sales on a first visit. Why? He is a master at no nonsense discovery. But best of all, Neal instinctively harnesses the power of NLP, called neural linguistics programming. While neural linguistics programming has been around some time, Neal takes it to a new level. When the customer leans forward, he leans forward. When they lean back, he leans back. When they pause, he pauses. His eye contact is superb and his body language always on target. Neal is a proponent of using just the right words at just the right time. One of his favorite closes is "Based on what we've shared together and the fact you've done your due diligence in seeking out your next home, how does this look to you?" (Trial close)

Customer says, "Just fine."

"Then, I'm hearing we've found your one-of-a-kind, is that correct?" (Test close)

Customer agrees.

"Then let's go ahead and make it yours, shall we?" (Final close)

The three steps of closing – Trial, Test, and Final – in proper sequence are the hallmark of a master closer. Neal's success is based on a process, but it is a process immersed in empathy for the prospect family.

TOM TALKS... About Commitment to Training

Rex of Centex reminded me of the time in Chicago when we were doing a major training and education program. A minor hurricane swept through the area. The rains came, the winds whipped, the trees were coming down, and all the power went off. Did that deter this venerable group? No way! We continued the training and education in a pitch dark, humidly oppressive room until we could no longer stand it. That's commitment to training survival and ultimately selling excellence.

U.S. Shell Homes

Self Prospecting is the Only Way

I was attending a Builder 100 conference several years ago when the president of Jim Walter Homes stood up to make a farewell speech to the industry. Jim Walter was a participant in the shell home business which was the darling of Wall Street back in the early to mid 60s. It was an interesting talk, but a bit out of the mainstream of today. When I heard him eulogize U.S. Shell Homes, my body became erect and my ears cocked. Why was he talking about this company? U.S. Shell was a small start up company with investors from New York that had bought a tiny shell home company in the South called Toney Builders. Through sheer salesmanship they became second in size to the mammoth Jim Walter. The retiring president went on that Jim Walter management could never understand how U.S. Shell Homes secured its business. After all, they ran no advertising, participated in no country fairs, did very little if any road side marketing, utilized no country bands or special promotions, and they sent out no direct mail. He revealed that U.S. Shell Homes almost reached the number one housing volume position in the U.S. on the strength of its sales staff.

After he was finished, I saw him at the coffee bar and introduced myself. "Would you like to know how U.S. Shell Homes procured their business?" I asked.

He answered, "Sure, after all these years, I'd be fascinated. Who are you?"

"I was vice president of sales and marketing for U.S. Shell Homes during that period of time, and I can explain in detail how we did it. Our goal was to become number one volume builder in the low income category. We figured we could not beat the giant Jim Walter with advertising dollars, so we elected to do it through our sales staff."

When I was brought on board by the two principals, I made a deal I would join the company only if they let me assemble a specialty sales team. By definition that is a team that generates its own business. It doesn't wait for advertised leads. With that understanding, we set forth to hire salespersons with legs, or the capacity to move away from a central location, go into the field, and generate their own business. We found many such sales people throughout the South, taught them how to find prospects by going into courthouses to see who had deeds to lots or land, showed them how to make an in-home presentation with a special

Visualizer kit that had been assembled by an ad agency in New York, and then we taught them the fine art of closing. Along the way, we had to teach them construction. It was one heck of a crew. They understood if they didn't prospect, they wouldn't eat. The mantra became, 'Prospect or Perish.' When a salesperson reached a certain volume for three months, we provided a leased automobile. When they reached the next level of volume, they were given a gas card. When they reached a third level of volume, incremental commissions jumped to help cover the costs of their time prospecting. It worked well. U.S. Shell Homes became the darling of Wall Street with its stock soaring to $74 on the New York Stock Exchange. Interestingly, to our knowledge, Jim Walter never sent spies into the organization and hence, never quite understood how we were doing it.

The bottom line was we paid the salespersons instead of an advertising budget. The sales staff prospered and worked hard – very hard. It was a seven day a week operation.

The sequel to the story is a novel one. Years later when U.S. Shell Homes was knocking on the door of the number one unit volume builder in the United States (remember our homes were priced at that time from $1,200 to $2,300 and the inside was totally u-finish). The New York Society of Security Analysts wanted a presentation about the shell home industry. It was a booming business. Shell Home stocks were soaring on the stock exchanges. What was this business? How did it conduct its affairs? What were the real profits? Was there viability in the building company or was it just a vehicle to produce loans for a finance company? These and many more questions would be answered by a tightly orchestrated presentation to this powerful group.

The day arrived. George Champion, the chairman of our board, led off with an overview of the financing aspect of the shell home business. Carl Knobloch, our company president, followed with an erudite explanation of how this business was an administrator's dream. He discussed empowerment to the branch managers, the profit centers each branch created, and the pro forma for sales and marketing. He emphasized that shell homes (a home where the interior is finished by friends and neighbors – some call it sweat equity) were the answer to low cost housing.

I was the third speaker. My job was to graphically show the analysts who we were selling these homes to, plus the bottomless market providing housing for the lowest of low income brackets. At this time, our profits were soaring and our customers were happy. We were providing new fresh housing opportunities for people who would not have had them otherwise. Villages, hamlets, and whole streets would turn out to help a buyer finish his home on the interior, so a lot of the value was labor created. It was a rewarding business! When I stood up to show slides of our buyers, some of those pictures were not pretty. Some showed poor, underfed, emaciated people living in Appalachia, the neglected folks of the Deep South – people in the hills of Tennessee and other areas that were living in the dire straits of minimal housing with leaky roofs and Swiss cheese walls. We were the answer to the under privileged portion of the U.S. population. Unfortunately, within minutes of my presentation, I saw the security analysts begin to bolt for the back door. The room was emptying out rapidly. I thought, is it me? Do I have the right audience? Am I saying something wicked? Then I realized that the "security" analysts had never seen this type of market before. These security specialists were running to telephones calling their principals to sell short all the shell home stocks they had in their portfolios! Mutual funds, pension funds, life insurance – everyone got in the act of selling shell home stocks short. In one day, there was a catastrophic collapse in the shell home industry. Our stock plummeted from $74 to $50 and kept going downwards. In fact, because of that presentation, the shell home industry was ruined. Strangely enough, it was a very good answer for people who could not afford conventional housing. The reality was that it was a good business. The perception was that it was not a sustaining business and they recommended dumping the stock. Life plays strange tricks.

The happy ending was, the entrepreneurial operators of the company took the financing arm and created a REIT, or real estate investment trust. Great American Mortgage Investors prospered for several years with the profits increasing each month. As it grew and grew, it became obvious that if things are too good to be true, then it's probably true. I sold my preferred stock and got out several months before the crash of the real estate investment trusts in 1974.

Another lesson here: Beware of paper profits. We saw this in the last Wall Street crash, and we may see it again. The real profits are made with real estate, and that is why we have the name "real" in real estate. While values are down, you must have enough facts to convince your customers that parking money in well located "use" property is an excellent place to put their money. Some day in the future, we'll look back and say, "I should have bought all the real estate I could get my hands on."

I would like to recognize the hard working men and women who comprised the U.S. Shell Homes sales team. For my money, it was the only large real estate sales staff I have seen that was totally dedicated to self-generation of sales through individual efforts. If we could take the housing industry which is too far removed from the self generation ethic and teach it networking through guerilla marketing methods, we'd have the best of all worlds. Call it Triple Threat salespersons: In football there are three "threats"; running, passing, and kicking. Arguably the last football player in the National Football League who did all three was Paul Hornung of the Green Bay Packers, but that was some years ago. Similarly, there are not many salespeople today that are accomplished at the three threats of selling. **Threat one** is generating your own traffic. **Threat two** is counselling and closing what comes on site. **Threat three** is the capacity to earn the referral sale on a continuing basis. When a sales person can exercise all three tenets in equal measure, that is a triple threat home salesperson.

TOM TALKS... About Funny Things on Resumes

To tickle your funny bone, here are quotes taken from actual resumes of salespersons or sales managers who will remain unnamed for obvious reasons.

"I am secretly writing to you, as I have written to the Builder 100 companies every year for the past three years for a sales job."

"Terminated after saying it would be a blessing to be fired."

"Wholly responsible for two (2) bankrupt builders."

"I truly enjoy the job of sales mangler."

"Failed my broker's examination with fairly high grades."

"Completed 11 years of high school."

"Overlooked all areas to ensure an overwhelming success."

"At the insistent and persistent urging of your competition, I am applying for a sales job."

"I have cleaned up my police report. It is available upon request."

Charles

The CQ Closes a Big Deal

An acquaintance had written the largest New York commercial real estate transaction in twenty years. It was a gigantic complex of buildings, and Charles' brokerage firm had the listing on it. We were sharing a house in Palm Beach, and New Year's was approaching. Seems a Japanese group had put a deposit on the complex in January and had been working all year to finalize the contract. However, the deal had to be closed before the end of the year or it was null and void.

Three days before the drop-dead date, Charles got word from his accountants in New York that the contract was $500 off to the benefit of the Japanese. It was all I could do to keep him from flying to New York and muck up the transaction. However, it worked out fine. A half day before the deadline, the glitch was discovered and the complex sale closed. Charles was a world class closer!

It was rumored Charles had a 2% listing fee and a 1½ % selling fee, or a combination thereof. Whatever it was, his cut was in the millions. So, I asked him what his close or CQ (Closing Question) was.

Without hesitation he said, "Back in January, just after I got the listing, the Japanese group came into my office. We took them on a whirlwind tour of the buildings and they were pleased with what they saw. At that point, they said they had to go back to Japan and work it out with their peers. So, here was my close. We were in my board room and I asked them to look at the phone on the conference table. I slowly said, 'You see that phone there?'

"They replied, 'Yes.'

"Well, gentlemen, I have this package out to a German combine and a Dutch syndicate, as well as several other movers and shakers. See that telephone on my conference table? The first one that calls me on that phone gets the deal. So, I suggest we all sit down; you call your partners in Japan, and let's see if we can put this under contract, fair enough?"

"They called Japan, got everyone out of bed, worked through the initial wordage, and signed a deposit receipt subject to engineering and a myriad of details."

"Was that really your close?" I asked.

Charles smiled, winked, and said, "What do you think?"

If true, the message of his story is when you ask – you get – whether it's a $100,000 home or a multi-zillion dollar commercial real estate deal!

THE HIERARCHY OF CLOSING

There is a sequence to closing that makes the process easy to understand.

1. Create the ***1-of-A-Kind***. This is done at the purchase target.
2. Ask the Closing Question or Questions. This is your call to action -- and should be executed only after you have created ***1-of-A-Kind***.
3. If rejected, regroup and restate the benefits of owning, and ask for the order again. Persistence pays off.
4. As needed, utilize your closing variables:
   - ❑ **Exercise closing techniques**
   - ❑ Ask the **C**losing **Q**uestion or **Q**uestions **(CQ)**.
   - ❑ **Switch the Scenario.** You may have closed on the right home, but something is left unclosed (like financing or school district). You must close all modules for the agreement to fly.
   - ❑ **Change the environment.** It may be appropriate to return to the site.
   - ❑ Close another day.
   - ❑ Introduce your partner to help facilitate the close.
5. Follow up until you exhaust all possibilities.

Lucy

Master of the Closing Question

Lucy was selling golf course property for the Monterey Country Club in the Palm Desert area. We were asked to assess the sales staff and spent three days on-site observing this excellent crew in action. At the time, this company enjoyed a 20-25% share of market in resort condominium sales. But, the developer wanted to increase share. We analyzed the sales force and discovered Lucy was writing considerably more sales than anyone else. The reason was she understood the difference between asking a closing question and making the closing statement.

The closing statement sounds like this: "Let me show you all the benefits this property will give you. After I do, I'm sure you will want to own it. (Salesperson explains the benefits). Now, let me review why it is important to buy it. (Salesperson explains the urgencies). Now that I've explained the uniqueness of this preferred property, let's talk about it and see if it fits your needs."

The closing statement never asks the buyers to make a home buying decision.

The closing question espoused by Lucy was very different: "Now that we've found your one-of-a-kind, let's make it yours, shall we?"

This is a question that causes ownership to transfer and a contract to be written. Salespeople are paid for asking closing questions, not making closing statements. Know the difference and see your sales improve.

TOM TALKS... About Hanging Tough

The great sportswriter, Grantland Rice wrote this verse ...

"When that one great scorer comes to mark against your name,
He'll mark not whether you won or lost,
But how you played the game."

In the business of home sales, we've changed the verse ever so slightly ...

"When that one great scorer comes to mark against your name,
He'll mark not how you managed to fail,
But only if you closed the sale."

Bonus Section

Lagniappe for the Learned

Parting Shots of Motivation and Education

Let's look at three stories of supreme motivation. One is about a building products sales rep, the next about a world class athlete, and the third about a Mestizo Indian.

Ladies and gentlemen, start your motivation engines.

Ed

Taking a Moon Shot

In the fall of 1979, I was training the Congoleum national sales team. We were delivering a program called, "How to Sell the Builder-Rez Market." It was a two day affair where we discussed the whole spectrum of how to identify the top builders, gain audience with the decision makers, deliver a world class presentation, close on product urgency, service the account, and eventually enlarge and enhance Congoleum's business and its profit picture.

We were at the subject of how to create a database of target business opportunities. The curriculum moved from home building firms to Realtors, bankers, utilities, mortgage companies, lumberyards, DIY outlets, and just about anybody or anything that influenced the purchase of resilient vinyl flooring.

To my right sat a veteran of the flooring sales wars. His name was Ed. Picture an elderly gentleman with a classic brown pin striped suit, white shirt, blue (for Congoleum) necktie, and impeccably shined shoes.

We reached the "how-to" segment and I suggested, "Let's all think outside the octagon, not just the box! Let's all reach higher than just routines, standards, and norms. Let's aim high! Let's reach for the stars … LET'S TAKE A MOON SHOT!"

We suggested that every sales professional in that room make a business call on the most unlikely target of opportunity – but a real opportunity that if realized, the results would be off the chart.

Ed said it so well at a banquet commemorating his 'moon shot.'

"I got to thinking seriously about the moon shot idea. What would be the single biggest, most difficult and yet possibly the most productive sales call in the universe – the Government Accounting Office! They purchase all the resilient vinyl for all the new and used government buildings world wide."

Ed continued, "It was early 1980. Ronald Reagan had just been elected president and a whole new administration was taking over. With some difficulty, I discovered who the new head of the GAO was. With trepidation, I arranged a fifteen minute appointment – 'fifteen minutes to the second,' his gatekeeper said. Obviously this man was swamped with new responsibilities. Would it make sense to call on him?"

Now for Ed's knockout punch. "I entered the head of the GAO's office and encountered a desk piled high with file folders."

"Hi, sit down, you only get fifteen minutes. Obviously you see I'm busy," the GAO official said.

Ed knew he had one chance and only one chance to get the official's attention. "If I could show you a way to purchase just one brand of resilient vinyl flooring and have it drop shipped to any location for any of your government buildings world wide – one brand, one source, one accounting – would that be of interest?"

Pause.

Ed continued, "The head honcho peeked above the mountain of paperwork and said, 'Damn interested!'"

After an hour and a half of fine tuning the details, Ed walked out with the single largest contract for building materials ever written at that time by one sales representative! A real testimonial to taking the moon shot!

Now, think hard. What's your moon shot?

Big Andy

You'll Be Back!

I remember Big Andy. He was about as tall as he was wide. And fast, boy was he fast. He could turn on a dime, pirouette like Nureyev, and turn handstands. Some hulk! A gazelle on fireplug legs dripping with power.

Big Andy played semi-pro baseball with the Stamford Paragons. Little note was made that he was captain of his college football team, Arnold College. Why? Big Andy was one helluva baseball player. Man could he hit. He could tattoo the ball blind with one smooth swing. And when he got under the ball, it was a towering inferno of a drive up, up, and away over the centerfield fence.

And could he handle the hot corner? Don't hit anything to 3rd base because the big guy would hip pocket it and throw you out by a mile. A slingshot of an arm! Surely, we all knew it was just a matter of time before Big Andy was discovered by a baseball scout and sent to the Big Show. Yankee Stadium was waiting for Big Andy!

Then it happened! The Paragons had a career season building. Six wins and zero losses. It was mid June when Big Andy announced he was invited to attend the Los Angeles Rams football tryout camp. He explained, "Since I captained the Arnold team, they'll pay my way to LA."

"Are you kidding?" we cried in unison. "Arnold didn't play any powerhouse teams. You'll get killed out there." With a voice of one we shouted, "If you go, you'll be back."

But Big Andy insisted, "At least I'll get to see California."

We all thought he'd forget about it, and anyway, if he goes, he'll be back.

The day was an early summer scorcher. We were on our way to our seventh victory. The Byrum Vets weren't too hot and the game was a piece of cake. After the blowout, we all assembled at the Byrum Tavern in Port Chester, New York where Big Andy remarked, flashing his toothy grin, "Got my tickets for LA," he said. "Goin' to California!"

"Hell, Andy, no way. You'll be killed out there. Forget this foolishness and stick around."

"No," he said. "It might be fun. It might be my only chance to see the Pacific Ocean."

Once again in booming crescendo we shouted, "You'll be back, you'll be back!" A couple of guys even laughed.

The last time I saw him as a mere mortal, his sizeable latissimus dorsi were leaving the tavern bound for a new world, the world of professional football. And the rest is history.

Big Andy played with the Rams for a couple of years and was traded to the New York Football Giants. And guess what? Yankee Stadium indeed became his home. He owned it year after year after year, prowling the turf from his defensive end position. Making impossible plays in ballet style made him famous. Big Andy put a stamp on the defensive end position that set the tone for future players. And, it has never been equaled.

Big Andy never came back!

The summer Andy left, the Paragons went on to have a world class year, losing just four games, while Andy was launching a career that eventually took him to the Pro Football Hall of Fame in Canton, Ohio.

I remember the day I visited the hallowed hall for the first time. I couldn't wait to find Andy's bronze bust among the greatest of the great. It was a week day. It was quiet. There was no one around. Silence hung heavy as I searched for Big Andy. And then I found him, just like he looked the day he left the Paragons and we all shouted, "You'll be back."

Reverently I reached out and touched the bust. Out loud I said, "Big Andy, you won't be back. Good goin' big guy!"

Walking away, I thought how many times someone has said to me, don't try, don't dream, don't achieve. "If you go, you'll be back."

Because of Big Andy Robustelli, I now know winners aren't afraid to try. Winners aren't afraid of the road back!

Charley

Don't Blow It!

I remember Charley. It was a long hot summer in 1952. I had gone west to seek summer employment. It was a recession year of sorts. There was little work, especially for sophomoric college kids. Through the oil towns I drove. Midland, Odessa, Big Spring, until finally I hit pay dirt in Hobbs, New Mexico. I hired on with an oil drilling outfit probably because the owner's daughter took a shine to me. We worked tower on the big rigs that bring in the big strikes. There was no Holiday Inn at Hobbs then, but I did get lucky! A steamer named Johnny Paolino and his wife, Billye, took me in. I was living the "life of luxury" in a steamer's out shack on an unpaved street in Hobbs, New Mexico, 617 East Humble Street to be exact. It was there in Hobbs I met Charley.

The first work day, we assembled in the yard to load up the drilling trucks and head off to who knows where to dress and drill those monsters, affectionately called "rigs." Charley was there wearing a pear of jeans that could truly walk the talk. Faded, filthy, fascinating – you know, the genuine article kind. And, boy if they could talk, what a tale they'd tell!

Driving to the fields, I found myself on the steely, cold truck bed sitting next to Charley, a tall, mawkish man with graying hair around the temples. He was wearing a black, ten gallon hat encrusted with mud, sporting a flapping gash in the front – probably from a bull's horn in Calgary, I reasoned. When the hat came off, a wide band of white skin clashed with his leathery, windblown countenance. Only a slight droop in the shoulders gave evidence that Charley was old in years, if not in attitude.

And then it happened! Out came a paperback book looking suspiciously like the stuff guys like Charley buy in adult news stores. What was Charley reading? Something sensual and sensational no doubt. The fact that he was reading seemed curiously odd to me. As the sun peeked over the horizon, Charley dove into the book as we pitched and yawed and sped to our destination. He read on to the pages of – Shakespeare's *Twelfth Night!*

After a draining, dusty morning working tower 75 feet off the ground, it was time for lunch. From a grimy, faded knapsack came another book, *Plato's Republic!* Charley spread eagled himself on the ground during his well-earned break and devoured the pages.

In New Mexico, the sun doesn't go gently down; it's suddenly gone, unmercifully bringing that stinging bite of night air. Charley was next to me again, and as we huddled together to avoid the chill, he said in a high pitched Texas twang, "Like to read, kid?"

"Yep," I said guardedly entering the conversation.

"What do ya read?"

"Oh, novels, sports, things for fun – when I have the time. And then there's all that required reading in college. You know, what I have to read," I answered.

"College!" Charley bellowed. "You goin' to college, kid?"

"Yep."

"Where?" he demanded to know.

"Oh, a place back East called Yale. You've probably never heard of it," I replied. As soon as the words slipped out, I wished I could call them back.

"Yale, Yale …" he said with tired eyes.

And now Charley hit hard. "Doggone it kid! Do you know how damn fortunate you are? Do you have any idea the chance you've got? Kid, are you taking this opportunity for granted?"

As the truck merged into the dark horizon, he told me about his quest for a break. Born illegitimate, he was left on a doorstep. A Mestizo family took him in and raised him with love, but little else. A tent. A shirt and jeans. Little food. No schooling. Charley was a roustabout at 12 years, a pipe fitter at 15, and a tower guy at 18 years. Once or twice he tried to get schooling, but hunger got in the way. Charley was homeless, not by choice, but by 'luck of the draw.' The old saw I'd heard so often now took meaning, "There, but for the grace of God, go I."

The long, hot summer wore on. Charley's books became numerous. With glee he'd read passages from Cervantes, Dante, Homer. And Charley got me reading too –

not because I had to, but because I wanted to. We read, and read, and read every break we had. We traded paperbacks. More Shakespeare, Voltaire, Balzac, Fenimore Cooper, Dickens. We even read *War and Peace*. What a joy! What a delight! What a summer! To discover an intellectual oasis in the sands of New Mexico was an unforgettable warp of time.

The day we parted, two men hugged, not the sort of thing oil-field tough guys do, but we hugged just the same. We knew we'd never see each other again. And yet, we knew that the final touch was for the ages. How well I remember Charley's parting words as he raised his withered hand and said, "Keep on readin' kid. You only got one chance, you know. Don't blow it!"

Then Charley was gone. A giant of a man. With a message that lives on, "You only got one chance you know. Don't blow it!"

Back in college I put the only photo of Charley I had on the corner of my desk. It was a picture of this intellectual giant in oil patch rags leaning against the "Daisy Buford No. 14" well. Whenever I was cramming for a quiz or a final exam, I'd look at the picture, take a deep breath, and say … "Charley, good buddy, this one's for you!"

So, tell your sales staff to honor their opportunity! Remind them they work for the best company, in the best industry, at the most prosperous time the world has ever known. And if they ever doubt America, ask them to show you a better place anywhere! And remind them also to pull a page from Charley's book and heed the sage's timeless words – "You only got one chance, you know. Don't blow it!"

Tom Talks ...

Building a Library of Home Demonstration Tips

Demonstration tips can be gathered in many ways: through shopping competing salespersons, reading selling and how-to books, networking with other professionals, and just plain creativity. Here are some fail safe demonstration tips to create value. The next time you demo a home, try these on for size.

1. Sequence the floor plan correctly. Start with the living areas first, put dining and living rooms in the middle, and always leave the master bedroom to the end. That way, you achieve a selling crescendo. A floor plan that suits a family contributes presence and purpose to their lifestyle.

2. Launch your presentation from the outside, not the inside, and start with questions. "Mary, would you kindly share with Jimmy and I what you like about the exterior of our home?" "Jimmy, would you kindly review for us what you like about the outside of this home?" Whatever the buyer's don't mention, the salesperson fills in with a checklist that emphasizes architectural themes, colors, textures & fenestrations, entries, windows for fun and function, and roofing design.

3. Learn where to stand in the room. To create space, stand with your customers at a position where the ceiling line runs up and away from the eye with light sources at your back.
4. To create space, try not to present the plan in the center of the room. Stand at the perimeters or sit where the sweeping vista is in front of the seating area.
5. If you must quote square footage, quote the larger number first. "This is approximately 16 feet by 10 feet or approximately 160 square feet." That sounds larger than a 10x16 room.
6. When learning a new model, write the dimensions of a room softly on the door jambs. When asked for an accurate number, refer to your notes.
7. Don't walk into small rooms. Sometimes, the sizing is not proper for three or more people. Learn to present the room from outside the space.
8. Get serious about presenting windows. Carry a lighter in your pocket and when asked if there are double paned windows, flick the lighter next to the window panes and you will see two flames confirming the double paned glass. Or, you can put a dollar bill in the window jamb and close the window upon it. Ask the buyers to pull out the dollar bill. If they cannot do it without effort or tearing the bill, that confirms your windows are tight.
9. Learn to utilize the G-L-A-M-O-R acronym for presenting bathrooms: The bathroom is glamorous. It has abundant

light sources. It has accessories and amenities you would see in houses costing thousands more. It has beautiful mirrors. It is **o**rganized. And, it is a **r**etreat. In short, it is a world apart yet minutes away from the rigors of the world.

10. "Let's stand behind my imaginary picture frame. What do you see when you look at this floor plan? You see exciting style and design that would only be present in homes costing many thousands of dollars more."
11. "Let's look at this sweeping vista from the entry. I'm sure you know the breaks in construction or niches in walls cost considerably more to build than a plain old box. Let's count the breaks in the architectural design and see how they lend drama and character to the floor planning, shall we?"
12. "Let's count the light sources in the kitchen, both natural and artificial."
13. The way to judge a good fit and finish is to look at the caulking around tubs and showers. Is it thick on one end and small on the other? Or, do the tile sizes get larger or smaller from the entry? That's the sign of a poor framing job!
14. "Let's open this cabinet door. I've stocked this cabinet with groceries. I'm not a homemaker, so let me ask you. If this kitchen were yours, how would you stock these canned goods, detergents, cereals, beverages, etc.?" Note: you cut your cans and boxes from the bottoms, not the

tops, then stock the kitchens at random. Asking a potential home buyer to tell you how she would organize her kitchen can be the first step toward a trial close.

15. If you have a home with a basement, use the lower level to sell your construction. Understand how to sell the five biggest construction points: 1) how the soil is prepared and how the slab or basement is poured, 2) benefits of the framing job, 3) everything about the electrical, 4) how is the waste or plumbing system utilized to work at peak efficiency? Include your GREEN or energy efficient program, 5) the finish, trim, and final polishing job.
16. As a bonus, don't forget to include any landscaping that comes with the purchase.
17. Remember there are seven types of generic space in a master bedroom called owner's suite: 1) visual space, 2) raised ceiling, 3) headboard, 4) alternate use space/entertainment wall, 5) possible indoor/outdoor space, 6) dressing/boudoir space (in Canada it's called en suite), and 7) storage space.
18. To create a feeling of quality, ask your customers to run their little finger over the mitered joint in a doorway. Point out how soft the joint is – an indication the painting contractor was advised to use fine grade sandpaper on all joints before applying the paint, another indication of quality.

19. Know your grades of lumber. If your company is using No. 2 grade for framing, point that out. Benefit, no sagging walls or popping sheetrock nails.

20. Know everything GREEN about your construction and be prepared to communicate it to your buyers. GREEN is huge.

21. Understand the five ways heat is lost or gained in the home. It helps you clarify energy efficiency. 1) proper caulking and sealing, 2) venting of the heat out of the attic, 3) insulation type, R-value, and proper installation, 4) size, type, and placement of windows, allude to passive solar, 5) HVAC (Heating, Ventilating, Air Conditioning equipment with a SEER rating at or above code)

22. On the overview understand there are five determinants to proper interior design: 1) space in the right place, 2) floor plan appropriate for the family, 3) zoning or room connections, 4) drama, 5) storage. Learn how to demonstrate these model by model.

23. When you demonstrate a field model under construction, carry a mounted floor plan with you. Often the framing stage confuses buyers because closets can look like bathrooms, and bathrooms like closets.

24. Always carry a mounted community map in the vehicle. Sit mom in the right front and dad in the right rear. She holds the community map as you commence the tour.

25. Use demonstration tools where possible: 1) A laser pointer to point out quality crown molding, 2) a 33-foot

framer's tape where the steel tape extends 16 feet and does not buckle. The tensile strength allows you to point out dimensions easier. 3) a space measurement tool which allows a laser beam to measure the width and length of the room, calculate the numbers and arrive at a square footage.

26. If a competitor has an exceedingly poor framing job, why not distribute levels or plumb bobs with the advice to measure other builders' walls in the area. Do not single out a particular builder or bash a competitor. Just say the sign of an excellent framing job is plumb walls. Then say, "Before you buy a home anywhere, come back and give us the last look."
27. Discuss the fact that your builder uses quality, warranted paint. Since the cost of a paint job is 15% material and 85% labor, wouldn't it be smart to use a warranted paint to prevent costly repaints? It is one reason your builder has selected a brand name of warranted paint instead of an off brand.
28. In a model home, always walk people outside even though the site is not the one they purchase. Sell the outdoor living room and ask the prospects if this yard were theirs, how would they use it.
29. Always use brand names. To recognize nationally advertised brand names lends credence to the local builder's name and often they have a warranty separate and perhaps longer than the builder's warranty. Names

like Whirlpool, KitchenAid, GE, Owens Corning, Kohler, Sterling plumbing, Andersen windows lend credibility to the purchase and only enhance the product.

30. Label or describe the home before you enter whether it's a furnished model or a field model. For example, "Jim and Mary, this is my four bedroom, two and a half bath plan. It's called the Augusta. It features the master down and the children's rooms upstairs with a large great room we call a family room. There is a patio on the leisure side which accentuates rear yard living and can be a blessing in this climate. The home prices here start at $400,000 and up. With FHA financing, this home can be acquired for $14,000 down and approximately $3,088 per month, principal, interest, taxes, and insurance – before Uncle Sam's tax deduction.

31. When demonstrating dining rooms, remember there are five possible impact points: 1) proximity of the dining room to the kitchen, 2) size: the space accommodates ten to twelve table settings. (Often a conventional dining room size cannot accomplish this unless you turn the table around and borrow space from the foyer for those few days a year when you need the additional space) 3) light sources, 4) wall for the break front with the antique plates, 5) finish and trim such as chair rails, and glamorous crown moldings, light fixtures, French doors, and butler's pantry. Dining rooms deserve to be demonstrated.

32. Always step into the garage. Make it a point that your garage in your model home is pristine clean. Remember the garage is often dad's room. Discuss where the workbench goes, access to the rear yard, light sourcing, wall space to hang tools, or recreation area for teenagers on rainy days.

33. Use the affirmative phrase, "There is more architectural styling on the leisure side of our homes than many builders put on the front of theirs." This is particularly true of golf course property. Differentiate with that phrase. Remember we sell the front of the home emotionally and the leisure side logically. The rear façade is where we point out gutters and downspouts, wide roof overhangs, exterior building materials such as stucco, brick, or Hardy plank, or accessories to enhance leisure side living such as gas hook ups or water outlets.

34. Some forgotten items to demonstrate in a kitchen: kick space under the cabinets, light source and view to the rear yard, size and depth of pantry, crown molding around kitchen cabinetry, adjustable shelving, back splash, drawers that are constructed to hold thirty pounds of flatware, your choice of stains and colors (know the names the manufacturers use for the colors), indirect lighting under cabinets, countertop space, electrical outlets, raised ceilings, sweeping vistas from kitchen throughout the home, choice of flooring, brand name of anything in kitchen where name is well known, type of lighting – fluorescent or incandescent and type of range

hood, fans, microwave, how large the oven is (holds up to a 40 lb turkey), sinks, countertop material, solid wood doors, not laminated pressboard, clerestory windows where applicable, and storage (open all cabinet doors)

35. Know the dimensions of furniture so you can mentally furnish a suite if necessary. Carry a tape measure to help facilitate this.
36. His and her lavatories at the appropriate heights and the possibility of a whirlpool tub
37. Quality of the hardware and cabinet pulls – stainless or brushed nickel?
38. Know your noise abatement measures
39. Hot water heater brand, features and benefits
40. Climate conditioning brand, features and benefits – how they exceed the competition

There are other demonstration points which could be brought to bear, but these are the major ones.

"If a builder has built a house for a man and his work is not strong, and if the house he has built falls in and kills the householder, that builder shall be slain."

~Code of Hammurabi

About Ego and Empathy: The Salesmanship Grid

In 1963 two Harvard professors wrote a learned treatise on the power of ego and empathy in selling. It made quite a splash in those days and became one of the first doctrines to help management measure sales proficiency. Just for fun, we have created a simple quiz of eighteen questions, the answers to which would allow one to plot their balance of ego and empathy on a chart. Let's see where you fall on the Salesmanship Grid.

Test Yourself!

		YES	NO
1.	If someone steps in front of you, do you ask him or her to step aside?	____	____
2.	Do you really try to concentrate on what someone tells you even if he or she's a bore?	____	____
3.	Do you get upset if you lose a sale and analyze why?	____	____
4.	Have you sometimes made a prospect mad?	____	____
5.	Are you sincerely touched by people with physical or mental challenges or even by crippled dogs?	____	____

6. During a routine or involved sales presentation, do you ask more questions than you give out information? ____ ____

7. Is it important for you to be #1 at everything you do? ____ ____

8. During a social conversation, do you feel put down when someone makes a wittier remark than you? ____ ____

9. Have you ever thought of yourself as "bashful?" ____ ____

10. Winning is everything. ____ ____

11. You're happy with yourself! ____ ____

12. Pleasing people pleases you. ____ ____

13. You get more pleasure closing a sale when you know people will benefit than you do earning the money. ____ ____

14. Children annoy you. Tell the truth! ____ ____

15. When someone talks in a drawl, do you purposely slow down? ____ ____

16. Sometime in past experience, have you talked your way out of a sale? ____ ____

17. I try to "look the part" of whatever endeavor I'm doing. ____ ____

18. When drivers try to get into the lane ahead of you, do you let them in? ____ ____

How to Score the Salesmanship Grid

*There is one "correct" answer.

* For example, the answer to question 1 is YES.

*If you circled "YES," give yourself one EGO point.

*If you circled "NO," you get **no points**.

The answers:

1.	Yes	EGO	7.	Yes	EGO	13.	Yes	EMP
2.	Yes	EMP	8.	Yes	EGO	14.	No	EMP
3.	Yes	EGO	9.	No	EGO	15.	Yes	EMP
4.	Yes	EGO	10.	Yes	EGO	16.	Yes	EMP
5.	Yes	EMP	11.	No	EGO	17.	Yes	EMP
6.	Yes	EMP	12.	Yes	EMP	18.	No	EGO

NOW, count the number of EGO points and count up vertically the corresponding number. Then, count the number of EMP (empathy) points and count across horizontally. Circle your location on the graph. This tells you your numerical standing on the Salesmanship Grid.

Salesmanship Grid

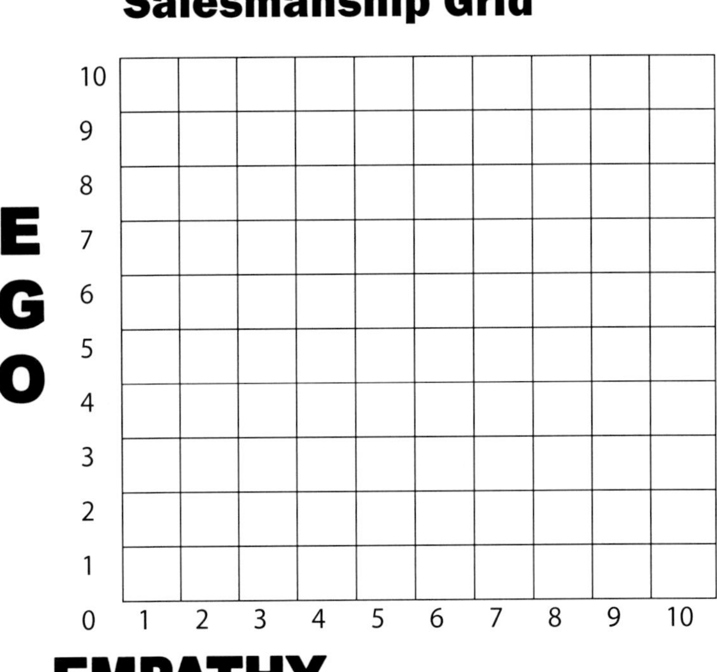

Although the quiz is too short to be definitive, there are lessons to be learned from this exercise for salespersons and sales managers.

If I plot myself in the lower left quadrant, I am probably a non salesperson *i.e.,* little ego and empathy. If I plot myself on the higher left quadrant, I have an ego drive that is out of balance with my empathy and, while I write many contracts, I have a high degree of cancellations. If I plot myself on the lower right quadrant, I have too much empathy and not enough ego to bring prospects to contract. I have low cancellations because I'm everybody's friend, but I also have low sales. If I plot myself on the upper right quadrant, I have a high degree of ego and empathy and am on the road to becoming a master closer. The best sales staffs possess a balance of ego and empathy. For example, I will do quite well in sales if I have 5 parts of ego drive and 5 parts of empathy.

Where did you fall on the Salesmanship Grid?

One other point: Having trained thousands of salespeople in my life, I truly believe the following.

5 out of 100 sales people are naturals. They are like natural athletes. They don't have to train, study, or diet to be great. It's a gift from God and they apply it to their chosen profession until they burn out!

10 out of 100 sales people should not be selling at all! They are a fish out of water. Their personality does not fit the job. They are left brain introverts that would rather be dealing with inanimate projects like computer programs than dealing with the maddening vagaries of people.

85 out of 100 sales people are learned. Through drilling, practicing, and rehearsing, and a reasonable level of applied skills, they become successful and are the bell weather of any industry. I'll take someone who has to work at it to be the core of my staff any day. Their attitude, trainability, and work ethic propels them to greatness.

Are You the Professional Who...?

Now, I ask you to find your special La-Z-Boy chair. Put it in the reclining position. Lean back. Play your favorite background music and ruminate (some call it room-inate when they demonstrate a model) and think about how many of these things you do in the course of a day or a week.

☑ Are you the professional who has a large flip chart behind their desk to work out numbers bold enough for the buyer to see, not buried on a small computer screen?

☑ Are you the professional who is fast and accurate with the numbers, and do you feel comfortable taking the buyer through an A to Z financing presentation? Then, tear off the flip chart page, fold it up, and give it to your buyers as a memory link to return.

☑ Are you the professional who has videoed the location benefits within a two to three mile radius? Have you collected the menus from the local restaurants? Do you know the hours of the health clubs? Can you answer any and all questions about your area in detail?

☑ Are you the professional who has a Visualizer presentation book on their desk or in the model and are you prepared to take the customer through the pages which best answer their questions?

☑ Are you the professional who has done your quarterly sales business plan and projected out your sales volume according to traffic sources?

☑ Are you the professional who has an organized "Reasons to Call Back" checklist next to the telephone?

☑ Are you the professional who has asked your construction superintendent to put a tape recorder around his neck and walk you through how the homes are built from the ground up? Then, take any unanswered questions on that tape to the expert for the answers.

☑ Are you the professional who has focused on learning the style and design of your different plans and exteriors? Can you stand in front of a model exterior and give a question driven presentation about the benefits of your architectural styling? For example: "Mary would you kindly share with Jimmy and me what you like about this exterior?" "Jimmy, would you kindly share with Mary and me what you like about this exterior?" Then, you fill in the points that they don't mention.

☑ Are you the professional that labels or brands the home before entering? For example: "Jim and Mary, this is our Heritage model. It's a four bedroom, 3½ bath, two story home with a large family room, open and informal kitchen and great room area, plus an additional room for a playroom or children's homework room. The base price is $450,000. With our special financing we can bring that in at about $3,500 per month. How does that sound?"

☑ Are you the professional who keeps abreast of the competitions' websites, makes hard copies of them, and puts them in a vinyl binder?

☑ Are you the professional who puts your name on t-shirts and water bottles to distribute to likely candidates?

☑ Are you the professional who makes feature and benefit flashcards of each room of your model homes – features on the front and benefits on the back?

☑ Are you the professional who gets manufacturers reps training you and talking about the U-benefits of their properties? For example: The electrical, plumbing, roofing, window, insulation contractors, to name a few.

☑ Are you the professional who reaches off site with your brochures properly placed at retail establishments?

☑ Are you the professional who prospects at military bases if they are within your marketing territory?

☑ Are you the professional who understands how to initiate a company sales generation program working with human resources, personnel directors, or small business owners?

☑ Are you the professional who has a magnetic sign on your vehicle?

☑ Are you the professional who engages a flatbed truck to drive 6x12 foot signs throughout the city to advertise your product? (The driver gives out brochures.)

☑ Are you the professional who writes a personalized community sales letter?

☑ Are you the professional who recognizes a "yard of the month" in your community?

☑ Are you the professional who works your 10 Points of Contact Referral Sale Matrix? Simply said, you have ten points of contact from the time you write the contract to one year from when the sale funds at which time you ask for a name, address, and phone number of folks in the market for a new home. Your goal is to strive for five viable leads which you then work as primary business sources. Goal – to write a minimum of one sale per buyer for the effort.

☑ Are you the professional who is truly serious about his or her follow up? Right now at this point, is your database up to speed? Is it reconciled, prioritized, and operable?

☑ Are you the professional who understands at this exact moment, how many "A" and "B" prospects are coming through your pipeline?

☑ Are you the professional who registers everyone who visits your community?

☑ Are you the professional who sends a food basket to Realtor offices with a thank you note and several company brochures after a sale is written?

☑ Are you the professional who is capable of giving a sales meeting for brokers on "How to Read Blueprints?"

☑ Are you the professional who speaks at the local Realtor educational meeting on the subject "How to Cooperate with Home Builders?"

☑ Are you the professional who knows how to solicit high end renters with a quid pro quo, *i.e.*, I'll send you prospects who can't qualify for my homes if you send me prospects whose leases are expiring.

☑ Are you the professional who knows how to work with cultural buyers? Are you up on the new financing for them?

☑ Are you the professional who puts your business card on corporate bulletin boards, retail store bulletin boards, or puts flyers in a parking lot with permission of the apartment manager?

☑ Are you the professional who radiates? That is asking everyone not purchasing from you if they know of anyone in the market for a new home.

☑ Are you the professional who has friends shop the competition so you know what they are saying about you?

☑ Are you the professional who really understands the new age and new criteria for fundamental home selling?

☑ Are you the professional who really motivates yourself with internal and external motivations?

For example:

INTERNAL MOTIVATION

- Read inspiring books/ listen to educational CDs and DVDs
- Look inward, measure strong suits, short suits, how to improve
- Listen to motivational music
- Rev up your positive mental attitude – PMA
- Set makeable goals: short, mid, and long term
- Construct a sales business plan
- Fill your pipeline
- Start a new hobby
- Embrace: "All you can do is the best you can do."
- Don't join the "whine and sleaze" party
- Give yourself 'attaboys'
- Set up a Rainy Day Fund
- Schedule a family trip
- Reward yourself with a shopping spree
- Create a tangible goal: new TV, new car, new wardrobe
- Lose one inch around your waist
- Clean your house
- Wash your car
- Collect a new close!
- Referrals motivate: Go get one!

EXTERNAL MOTIVATION

- Work to the M-O-T-I-V-A-T-E formula: Earn more **M**oney ... get **O**rganized ... self **T**rain your short suits ... **I**nvolve yourself in self improvement ... employ the **V**ictorious attitude ... **A**pprobate yourself ... give **T**LC to other people. Get **E**nergized, **E**nthusiastic, **E**mpowered!
- Be proud of your victories and accomplishments
- E-mail congratulations to friends and clients
- Enthusiastically embrace a sales training program
- Buy tickets for a show or cultural event
- Participate constructively in the Planned Encounter
- Sell the concentration home
- Visit competitors' communities (to reinforce your value)
- Hold breakfasts for Realtors
- Win a contest
- Get a role model. It's OK to have one.
- Hold a BBQ for your owners. Tell them to bring their friends.
- Collect plaques and trophies
- Treasure your compliments
- Eat right!
- Do a little exercise every day
- Create a future event you can look forward to

"You sell good when you feel good – Success starts from within." *~Tom Richey*

30 Ways to Whip the Market!

1. **Register 10 or more new prospects weekly**

   Solution: Self generation and use of a "People I Know" worksheet *(The Richey Self Prospector)* *(see page 18)*

2. **Create new ways to bond and connect**

   Solution: The more you sit, the more you fit. Ask more questions.

3. **Embrace question-driven counselling**

   Solution: Smell out the buyers' agenda with questions, then close to their needs and wants.

4. **Cut to the chase of affordability**

   Solution: Ask qualifying questions. Do a financing set up.

5. **Use the 'Rule of DDS' when handling objections**

   Solution: Learn to overcome Dollars, Distance, Size, School, Security objections and the "Squeal for the Deal"

6. **Make closing easy**

   Solution: Soft multiple close with gentle persistence

7. **Service with passion**

   Solution: Goal! To earn the referral sale

8. **Write more referrals**

   Solution: Use the 10 Points of Contact Matrix. Strive for 5 names and addresses and phone numbers. Follow up on them!

9. **Organize a SWAT team of cooperating brokers**

Solution: Put 10 VIBs (Very Important Brokers) into your stable. Convert to VIP's (Very Important Producers) when they sell a home.

10. **Prepare to sell**

    Solution: Organize your toolbox with a Visualizer book – and learn your product!

11. **Know your competition!**

    Solution: Pull a comparison worksheet at least quarterly

12. **Eliminate cancellations**

    Solution: Sell the home right the first time and do a CBA (cost breakdown analysis)

13. **Enter the world of social networking**

    Solution: Acclimate yourself to Facebook, YouTube, Twitter, and blogging (Don't be a social notworker)

14. **Brand yourself**

    Solution: Give out 50 business cards a week … Put a magnetic sign on your car and create your own website

15. **Keep accurate records**

    Solution: Stay on top of your database and Focus & Accountability worksheets

16. **Set best effort goal of one sale per week**

    Solution: Focus on "most sold" prospect(s)

17. **Heed the Power of the Lost 19**

    Solution: If you close one of twenty, what happened to the 'lost 19?'

18. **Learn how to sell and close with your financing**

    Solution: Buy Tom Richey's 'Home Sales Financing Handbook'

19. **Beef up your construction knowledge**

    Solution: Train with your construction superintendent and use a construction quality worksheet

20. **Value differentiate your counselling**

    Solution: Ask twice as many questions as you give out information. Create a product differentiation worksheet. Include financing, location, and lifestyle

21. **Fine tune your IT selling process**

    Solution: Work to convert web visits to site tours

22. **Push your personal training envelope**

    Solution: Work into a formula of checklists, worksheets, practice sessions, books, CDs, DVDs, and shop the competition. Get a network of non competing peers. Attend seminars. Join your home builders association.

23. **Stay motivated. Live positive!**

    Solution: Write up a personal PMA kit. What motivates the motivator (you)?

24. **Get creative!**

    Solution: Cross sell through new and resale disciplines. Cross pollinate equities, processes, and powers

25. **Don't participate in recession mongering**

    Solution: Stay the course. Someone in your market is selling homes.

26. **Demonstrate to create true value for true price**

    Solution: Focus on selling and closing with financing, construction differentials, and style and design essentials

27. **Follow through on all requests**

    Solution: Keep follow up system suitably logged and prioritized for instant action

28. **Learn how to neutralize the negotiator**

    Solution: Commit the neutralization method to a well rehearsed storyline

29. **Networking is the new business generator**

    Solution: Organize two lists: one for primary buyers and the other for influencers. Work the sales influencer category consistently.

30. **Fashion a P-R-O-F-I-T formula**

    Solution:

    Present to 2010 criteria.

    Rs generate sales: Realtors, Referrals, Radiation, Repeats, Renters, Retailers, Residuals, Response

    Organize your time and efforts

    Follow up

    Initiate the close

    Train to sell a cut above and a step ahead

A Magic Carpet Ride ...

Let's take a magic carpet ride across the United States and see what the great salespeople are doing now ...

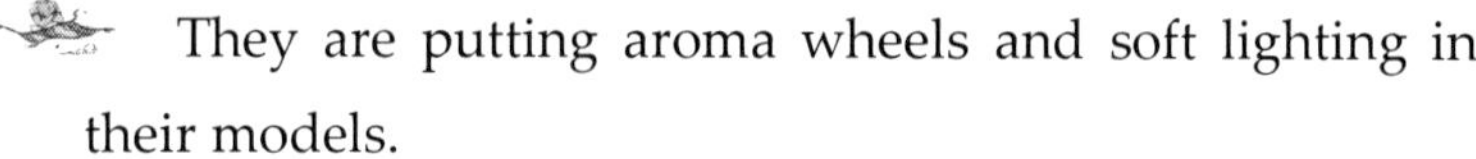

- They are putting aroma wheels and soft lighting in their models.
- They are saying, "Join our 100 Foot Club" when they have broader frontage than the competition.
- They are sprucing up their sales offices so they don't look like Burger King after the noon rush!
- They are selling with pristine clean models, spotless garages, and all closets free of clutter.
- They have a highly effective Visualizer presentation book. The book has five sections: 1) happy owner letters, 2) 'why buy now' articles, 3) sales office displays reduced to scrapbook size, and 4) information on the three biggest competitors, 5) financing worksheets
- They have financing thumbnails on at least six individual family loan qualifications in their Visualizer.
- They are working toward 100% referrals – which means one sale for every one new home sold. They consider their owners prime influentials for generating business.
- They are using the *Real Estate Master IIIx* calculator in the field for credibility.

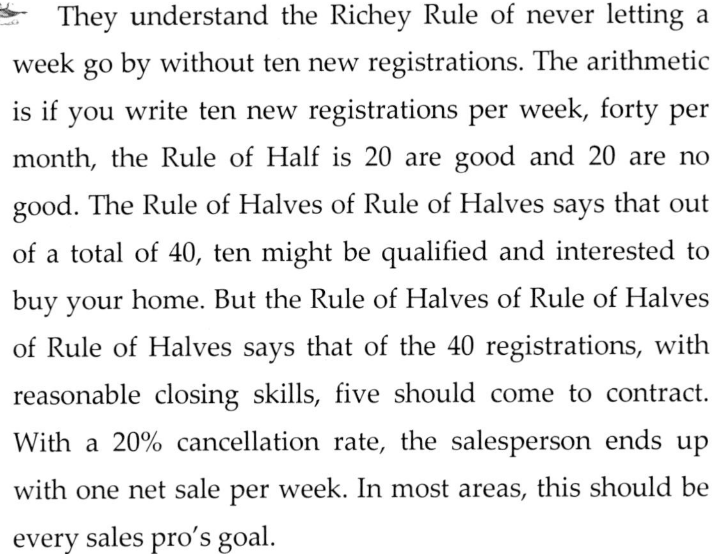

- They understand the Richey Rule of never letting a week go by without ten new registrations. The arithmetic is if you write ten new registrations per week, forty per month, the Rule of Half is 20 are good and 20 are no good. The Rule of Halves of Rule of Halves says that out of a total of 40, ten might be qualified and interested to buy your home. But the Rule of Halves of Rule of Halves of Rule of Halves says that of the 40 registrations, with reasonable closing skills, five should come to contract. With a 20% cancellation rate, the salesperson ends up with one net sale per week. In most areas, this should be every sales pro's goal.

- They have a toolbox which contains a 100 foot tape measure, Visualizer, mounted floor plans, digital and Polaroid cameras, Ziploc bags, box-type clipboard to hold paperwork, eight colored cones, and mounted plats.

- They are going off site to follow up on stubborn prospects or to cultivate influentials.

- They are taking one day off a week and using it to generate prospects away from the site, often writing call reports back to sales management.

- They understand that nothing happens until one asks for the sale ... and they know that 80% of all big ticket sales are made after the fifth close!

- If they find out the competition is bashing their builder, they ask the prospects to take a five minute presentation at their builder's quality display wall before entering the models. This pays off in selling the vitamin Cs of Confidence and Credibility.

- They understand the basics of guerilla marketing and do a little prospecting every day.

- They understand the power of coun<u>sell</u>ing with financing, construction benefits and style and design.

- They are focusing on the differentiations of style and design so much, they are calling themselves the "architects of style and design."

- They are exercising the coun<u>sell</u>or's credo: "Whether you buy a home from me or somebody else, there's information you need to have to make an informed decision."

- They order educational books and listen to CDs, always raising their bar of expertise.

- They are using Internet training opportunities wisely and consistently.

- They are using tape recorders to practice and fine tune their presentations

- They are constantly updating their financing knowledge.

- . They start the day with "Good morning, God" – not, "Good God, it's morning!"

Take a look. Selling magic is happening all around you.

Are you part of it!

Closing Truisms from a Closer

Closing is when preparation and opportunity collide.

Closing is not a moment in time!

There's no tomorrow if the prospects meet a closer on the way home!

The prospects usually have one more objection than you have a close!

Demonstration begets PROFITUATION not SCHMOSITUATION

Always ask 5 closing questions!

Over-finessing leaves you guessing!

Save your biggest urgency shot until the end.

When your prospects slip through the crack, follow up will bring them back!

Closing is democracy in action!

~Tom Richey

A Final Exhortation

Every home salesperson should have a Visualizer presentation book. It is a sales tool – much like a scrapbook – that facilitates sales points. For example, the first section is comprised of happy home owner letters, notes, and e-mails. The second section is "Why Buy Now" articles. The third section is sales office displays reduced to presentation book size (usually 11x17 inches). The fourth section is information on the salesperson's three biggest competitors. These presentation books are portable, can rest on a stand, and help make sales points with graphic sales power. They are an integral part of every toolbox. Years ago, Winchester Homes had a Visualizer creation contest. Each salesperson was asked to make a Visualizer that left nothing to chance in the closing module. The winning Visualizer was ingenious.

The sales professional procured a copy of a ten year old Winchester advertisement for a condominium project in Manassas, Virginia. The headline promoted prices under $200,000. Then, he constructed a page highlighting his present ad, Manassas condominiums for $400,000. The third page was a Kiplinger report projecting prices ten years ahead. The salesperson's dialogue ran like this …

"I understand you feel the prices of my condominiums are too high, is that correct?"

Prospect says, "Yes."

"Please look at this ten year old ad. Back then people were also saying prices were too high. But I bet you'd buy one today at the $200,000 number, am I right?"

Prospect says, "Absolutely."

Salesman continues, 'Now, here's my current ad. You are saying you can qualify for the loan, but $400,000 is too high, right?"

"Yes."

"OK. Look at this survey by Austin Kiplinger. Despite what you hear about lowering values today, Kiplinger predicts prices will escalate to at least $600,000 in this area ten years from now! So, it's all relative. Buy now and pay yourself the different between $400,000 and $600,000! Makes sense, doesn't it? Let's go ahead and do the paperwork, shall we?"

This was a world class presentation that worked in the real world!

Finally, take this exhortation and paste it on your make-up or shaving mirror. Refer to it daily and put its message to work.

> *"I shall not rest until I and my community are selling up to speed!"*

SELLING AND MARKETING CODE OF ETHICS FOR THE U.S. HOUSING INDUSTRY

Preamble

No product brings stature and stability to the families of this great nation more than the fulfillment of the American dream of home ownership. It is the responsibility of all new home salespersons, marketers, and builders to honor this right through adherence to the highest standards of professionalism, morality, and dignity. With this mantle of responsibility comes the total commitment to excellence as reflected in this Code of Ethics. In order to raise the level of selling conduct and expertise, these sales principles are willfully adopted and endorsed by housing sales and marketing professionals.

Code of Ethics

1. To be informed in and uphold the spirit of all federal, state, local laws, ordinances, and governmental regulations pertaining to consumer protection and equal housing opportunities.
2. To refrain from any statement, promotion, or advertisement that is deceptive, unethical, or fraudulent, and from the use of implications or half-truths that could falsely represent a proposition.
3. In all advertising, promotion, and in the sales of new or resale homes, to accurately and honestly describe the inclusions, materials, price and terms, quality of workmanship, and hidden values of construction without exaggeration and in the clearest possible language.

4. To keep buyers informed during the construction and/or loan approval process and communicate in writing any variances from the norm with dispatch prior to closing.

5. To conduct the business of selling and marketing in a manner that will reflect credit upon the housing industry: builders, Realtors, lenders, manufacturers, and all associated marketing disciplines.

6. To make full disclosure of any adverse factors in construction or neighborhood nuisances which might affect the value and desirability of a home.

7. To continually strive to acquire updated knowledge of the housing industry and the latest selling skills and marketing methods, and to freely share this information with fellow professionals through local and national association events.

8. To avoid controversies by respecting the integrity of competing home building firms, and to refrain from seeking unfair advantage through questionable sales or marketing practices.

9. To neither encourage nor accept compensation from a third party unless such compensation is permitted by law and executed with the full knowledge of all parties. In addition, to protect and hold sacred in a special account any deposit or down payment monies received on behalf of the client.

10. To furnish each party to a transaction an accurate copy of the sales agreement insuring that all financial obligations and product commitments are completely understood and agreed upon.

11. To absolutely refrain from divisive, political, prejudicial, or pejorative statements that would bring harm to the housing industry.

12. To be fair and equitable in all matters relevant to selling and marketing the American Dream.

Richey Resources Skills Enrichment Library ...

The Essential New Home Sales Manager's Handbook

842 pages, hard cover resources book on selling and sales management filled with readers, forms, and checklists every manager needs to effectively staff, recruit, select, train, motivate, and monitor the sales staff.

Home Sales Financing Handbook

252 pages, soft cover. The industry's first book on how to sell and close with your financing. Learn about loans, mortgages, types of financing, helping the buyer find the money for a down payment, helping the buyer deal with a house to sell, and so much more.

Counselling the Mature Lifestyle Home Buyer

Hardbound, 334 pages setting out the processes and procedures needed to successfully sell to the 55 Plus home buyer. They are sold differently than buyers in the conventional market. So, who are these buyers? 55 Plus buyers purchase for primary residence, future retirement, or a vacation experience. Enter the 55 Plus salesperson who must coun*sell* and close this super consumer. Surveys show that liking and trusting the salesperson is one of the top three reasons they buy. Today, we no longer sell by chance, we sell by plan, and this book provides the plan.

The Sales Power of P.R.O.B.E.$

258 pages, hard cover book where you will find what you need to be successful in today's housing market. Many potential home buyers suffer from TMI or too much information. They get confused by conflicting claims and aberrant selling philosophies. Richey sorts it all out and reduces home selling to a simple process of JEI – or just enough information. A must read for new hires, seasoned professionals, or industry support personnel.

Lamar Hunt and the Founding of the American Football League

210 pages, hard cover book about the beginnings of the American Football League and the man who made it happen against insurmountable odds. At a time when the NFL owners had forged a monopoly and had rejected his offer to bring a team to Dallas, he shook the establishment by starting his own league. Professional football would never be the same!

Practical Applications Kits

Spiral bound flashcards with approximately 60 pages covering the major topics of today's new home selling process:

Style & Design – Checklists of items you

should consider on every presentation from architecture to sequencing, to interior design.

Time Management – Exercises which will help you arrange and transform your time into super productive time.

How to Neutralize the Squeal for the Deal and Close Sales with Your Financing – 100 absolutely indispensable rules of selling in a viciously competitive and voraciously profit-consuming market. CD available.

How to Write More Sales with Your Financing – All you need to know about mortgages, types of financing, types of loans, helping the buyers qualify, and more.

Selling New Homes in a Tough Market – Fundamental and advanced selling processes that must be used to bring today's often contrary buyer to a decision.

Checklists for the New Home Sales Counsellor – Covers Discovery, Demonstration, Questions & Phrases, Style & Design, Toolbox creation, Closing, Urgency, Buyer Characteristics, and the total presentation

ASK ABOUT OUR WORLD CUP OF SELLING EVENT!

All books and resources are available for purchase at

www.richeyresources.com

Tom Richey, MIRM, CAASH

Tom Richey, NAHB's 2006 *Legend of Residential Sales & Marketing*, has worked tirelessly in the housing industry for over 50 years and offers that experience to those in the housing business via on-site sales training, marketing consulting, or through internet methods such as webinars and networking events.

Richey, founder and president of Richey Resources, Co. is a long time champion of the front line new home salesperson and sales manager. Richey has seen and experienced just about every up and down the market can throw at the housing industry. Tom has helped builders of all sizes across the country fine tune their sales and sales management staffs to a higher standard of excellence. Richey created the first national video conference sales rally, originated National Housing Week which began in 1980, developed the nation's first salesperson's mystery shopping program, marketed the first high rise condominium in the U.S., was Chairman of the National Sales and Marketing Council of the National Association of Home Builders, and so much more.

If you would like to receive sales or sales management training from the primary source, please call us at 800.346.3354; e-mail to tom@richeyresources.com; or write to Richey Resources, 1616 S. Voss Road, Suite 820, Houston, TX 77057.

www.richeyresources.com